Praise for *A Witch*...

"At a time when so many books on magick focus only on a narrow modern approach, Melanie Marquis has given us a fascinating overview of tried and true magickal techniques from around the world since the beginning of time. This book is the perfect jumping-off point for expanding your own work to encompass universal practices and principles of magick, melding the old and new with grace and power."

—Deborah Blake, author of *Everyday Witch Book of Rituals*

"[A] unique and educational piece of work... This thought-provoking mixture of history and artistic practicum is designed to get the gears turning and empower fellow seekers to actively create magick rather than do it by-the-book. If you're looking to expand your spiritual practice and learn solid global wisdom, this relevant book is for you."

—Raven Digitalis, author of *Shadow Magick Compendium*

"A delightfully fresh and incisive look at magick from around the world and throughout the ages. Each chapter begins with the clarity and precision of the scholar's eye. However, unlike other works that merely repeat what was printed before, Marquis then examines the information looking for underlying similarities that will allow the practitioner of today to actually use the techniques rather than simply read about them."

—Donald Michael Kraig, author of *Modern Magick*

"Melanie has sought out various practices from different cultures from all over the world during different eras... I am confident that all eclectic practitioners will find at least a few new techniques that will challenge them, leading to fresh growth and development."

—Tony Mierzwicki, author of *Graeco-Egyptian Magick*

Praise for *The Witch's Bag of Tricks*

"*The Witch's Bag of Tricks* is a great read. It has an amazing number of those tricks along with good, solid advice and information. Old Witches and new can benefit from this book. I heartily recommend it."

—Raymond Buckland, author of
Buckland's Complete Book of Witchcraft

"[A] great way to bridge the gap between beginning and intermediate witch-craft studies. Filled with techniques and tricks most practitioners may or may not learn over time, Marquis addresses quite well the single biggest trip-up to most would be casters: the magical mindset…Highly recommended."

—Diana Rajchel writing for *www.FacingNorth.net*

a
WITCH'S
WORLD
OF
Magick

Photo by Andrew Harris

About the Author

Melanie Marquis is a lifelong practitioner of magick, founder of the United Witches global coven, and organizer of Denver Pagans. She's the author of *The Witch's Bag of Tricks* and has written for national and international Pagan publications, including *Circle* and *Pentacle Magazine*. She also writes for several of Llewellyn's almanacs and datebooks.She resides in Colorado. Visit her at http://www.melaniemarquis.com.

To Write to the Author

If you wish to contact the author or would like more information about this book, please write to the author in care of Llewellyn Worldwide, and we will forward your request. Both author and publisher appreciate hearing from you and learning of your enjoyment of this book and how it has helped you. Llewellyn Worldwide cannot guarantee that every letter written to the author can be answered, but all will be forwarded. Please write to:

Melanie Marquis
℅ Llewellyn Worldwide
2143 Wooddale Drive
Woodbury, MN 55125-2989

Please enclose a self-addressed stamped envelope for reply,
or $1.00 to cover costs. If outside the USA, enclose
an international postal reply coupon.

Many of Llewellyn's authors have websites with additional information and resources. For more information, please visit us at: www.llewellyn.com.

Melanie Marquis

a WITCH'S WORLD OF MAGICK

Expanding Your Practice
with Techniques &
Traditions From
Diverse Cultures

Llewellyn Worldwide
Woodbury, Minnesota

FIRST EDITION
First Printing, 2014

Book design by Bob Gaul
Cover art:
   1554377:iStockphoto.com/LeitnerR, 3374582:iStockphoto.com/janrysavy,
   305688:iStockphoto.com/dsteller, 19766604:iStockphoto.com/ollo,
   13427522:iStockphoto.com/de-kay, 18444070:iStockphoto.com/Corben_D,
   16428972:iStockphoto.com/mammamaart, 16428981:iStockphoto.com/mammamaart,
   219213:iStockphoto.com/Morrhigan, 20475123:iStockphoto.com/gavran333,
   2730309:iStockphoto.com/jeffreeee, 8556532:iStockphoto.com/CreativeFire,
   5026862:iStockphoto.com/Susan Trigg, 65251777:sniegirova mariia/Shutterstock,
   3209759:Vladimir Melnik/Shutterstock
Cover design by Kevin R. Brown
Editing by Laura Graves

Llewellyn Publications is a registered trademark of Llewellyn Worldwide Ltd.

Library of Congress Cataloging-in-Publication Data
Marquis, Melanie, 1976–
  A witch's world of magick: expanding your practice with techniques &
traditions from diverse cultures/Melanie Marquis.—First edition.   pages cm
  Includes bibliographical references and index.
  ISBN 978-0-7387-3660-0
1. Magic. 2. Witchcraft. I. Title.
  BF1621.M374 2014
  133.4'3—dc23

                          2013037369

Llewellyn Publications
A Division of Llewellyn Worldwide Ltd.
2143 Wooddale Drive
Woodbury, MN 55125-2989
www.llewellyn.com

Printed in the United States of America

This book is lovingly dedicated to my magickal mama Eva Janice Marquis, and to Franchesica Middleton and all the other wonderful witches who choose to make their own way in the world.

Contents

Acknowledgments   *xi*

Introduction   *1*

One: No-Tools Body Magick   7

Two: Potion Making and Mixing Magick   29

Three: The Art of Containing Energies:
Magick to Have and to Hold   51

Four: Ties that Bind   69

Five: Nail It Down: Insert Magick Here   81

Six: Naming Names: Identification in the Magickal Arts   97

Seven: Decoy Magick   111

Eight: Cursebreaking and Countercharms: Magick to Undo   129

Nine: Masks, Mimicry, and Magick   163

Ten: Group Magick   181

Bibliography   *203*

Index   *215*

Acknowledgments

Special thanks to my family and friends for the love and laughter that makes my world a magickal place. Mia, Aidan, Andrew Harris, Jon Marquis, Melissa Chapman, Elizabeth Bridges, Jenny Edwards, Eugene, Tavarius, Calvin Carter, Ahoono, and Sally, you all are the best and I thank you!

Introduction

With all the stigma and misconceptions still associated with modern witch-craft practice, it's easy to forget sometimes just how ancient and widespread the belief in magick truly is. Magick is arguably both older and more broadly practiced than many of the earth's most prominent organized religions. While Christianity dates from around 30 CE and boasts 2 billion follow-ers—an impressive tally, to be sure—magickal belief has its origins tens of thousands of years earlier and its traces can be found in nearly every culture on earth.[1] Anthropologists have yet to discover a primitive society completely devoid of beliefs that could be categorized as "supernatural"; among modern peoples, "superstitious" (aka magickal) practices such as knocking on wood to divert bad luck or carrying a lucky charm are sur-prisingly common. A recent poll indicated that 51 percent of Americans consider themselves at least somewhat superstitious, while a similar survey in England revealed even higher numbers.[2]

---

1   "Big Religion Chart," Religious Facts, accessed February 10, 2013, http://www.religionfacts.com/big_religion_chart.htm.

2   "Superstitions: Why You Believe," CBS News Sunday Morning, accessed February 8, 2013, http://www.cbsnews.com/8301-3445_162-57541783 /superstitions-why-you-believe/.

We can add to this the abundance of people around the planet who engage in magickal practices categorized and legitimized as "folk religion." Practitioners of indigenous Chinese religion, for instance, who number an approximate 394 million, frequently practice divination, astrology, and longevity alchemy. While these activities are practiced in a primarily religious context, they nonetheless have a quality that is easy to recognize as distinctly magickal. Consider also the 5 million followers of New Age philosophy, the 1 to 3 million Wiccans, and the masses of hard-to-count Neo-Pagans, chaos magicians, ceremonial magicians, hedge witches, kitchen witches, and undefinable others whose practices involve at least some form of magickal ritual, and you've got a good case for the worldwide prominence and popularity of magick.[3]

It's no wonder magickal practice is so widespread. It has a long history, and besides, magick *does* often work, after all. Archeologists have uncovered ample evidence of ritualistic burial practices, "venus" fetishes, and other relics that support a very early belief in magick and mysticim. The most conservative estimates date the time of humanity's first foray into ritual to at least 35,000–40,000 years ago, but more recent research points to an even earlier birth of magick.

In 2006, University of Oslo archeologists Sheila Coulson and Neil Walker released their findings about a ritual site located in an area of the Tsodilo Hills in Botswana that's estimated to be around 70,000 years old. Known as Rhino Cave, the cavern contains a large (20' by 6.5'), very snakelike rock, "Python Rock," which bears hundreds of human-made scorelines, grooves that resemble a pattern of scales. Beneath the snake, the archeologists unearthed hundreds of spearheads that seemed to have had a special, likely magickal, purpose. They're made from finer stones than the everyday spearheads of the time, more brightly colored and crafted from stones brought from up to 100 kilometers away. The cave shows

---

3   "Big Religion Chart," Religious Facts, accessed February 10, 2013,
     http://www.religionfacts.com/big_religion_chart.htm.

evidence that the spearheads were crafted on site, perhaps begun in another location, but finished right there at the side of the great snake.

Another interesting point about the spearheads reveals the subtlety and variance of magickal methods far into the distant past. Of the hundreds of spearheads that have been found at Python Rock in all their array of colors, only spearheads of a certain type show signs of having been placed in contact with fire. These spearheads have taken on a red color from the heating process, which was apparently a quick trip through a very hot flame. This heating action was different than the process typically used for tempering spearheads, indicating that these particular spearheads may have been burnt for a ritualistic, rather than practical, purpose. Other spearheads discovered at the site do not show any signs of burning. Fragments of quartz crystal were also found at the cave site, stuffed into cracks and crevices in the cavern walls and floor, and even stowed right beneath the giant stone snake.[4] If the dating on the Rhino Cave site is correct, this evidence taken together makes it appear likely that humans were exhibiting an understanding of magickal principles as far back as 70,000 years ago!

Although we'll probably never know the exact date of the origin of magickal ritual, one thing is clear: humans have been practicing magick for tens of thousands of years, and it seems that our magickal understanding has been fairly sophisticated from the get-go.

Like the recognized religions of the world, magick reflects an established (yet ever-evolving) belief system. There may not be a centralized dogma or a single, sanctioned set of explanations of phenomenon, but all the same, the arts of magick have indeed preserved and conveyed for ages an implied understanding and acceptance of certain universal principles on which nature and the rest of the world operate. We see in all magickal

4   Brian Handwerk, "'Python Cave' Reveals Oldest Human Ritual, Scientists Suggest," *National Geographic News*, December 22, 2006, accessed August 1, 2012, http://news.nationalgeographic.com/news/2006/12/061222 -python-ritual.html.

acts, for instance, the belief that our conscious intentions and symbolic actions can sway the inner workings of the world around us. We see the belief in the power of nature, human, and deity to influence reality, and we can identify also the assumption that the elements of this reality are interrelated, connected by an invisible web of energy that can be accessed and manipulated through thoughts, emotion, symbol, or correspondence. Whatever the outward appearance of our magick might be, the inner workings of the act are similar throughout the world.

By looking for these similarities and locating the common core of the tried-and-true, we discover new ways to view our own practices and gain fresh insights into the many ways an effective act of magick can be achieved. Our magick need not be restricted by tradition, but rather can benefit from being inspired and informed by it. This is a book of magick from around the world, illustrating time-honored practices and finding common threads with which to weave our own modern spells.

How to Use This Book

In each chapter, you'll find examples of tried-and-true magickal techniques from around the world. By getting more familiar with some classic "magickal moves," you'll have a solid starting point for designing your own mystical innovations. These examples are drawn from different cultures in different eras, highlighting the universality of various magickal principles. As you examine these methods, think about the underlying theories and beliefs exhibited in each unique act of magick. Repeating patterns and commonalities soon become apparent, and the eclectic witch can therein find a strong foundation on which to craft his or her own effective brand of magick.

You'll also find in each chapter a customizable spell to try along with other ideas for applying each magickal principle in a modern context. Each chapter also contains a section titled "Common Threads and New Perspectives," included to draw attention to significant commonalities in theory and technique applied by magick workers around the world. As you examine these common threads, do so with a critical mind and an inquisitive heart. I may very well be off about some things; you should trust in your intuition, judgment, and powers of reason to form your own best theories. Theories are meant to evolve, after all, and while I certainly might have some of the answers, you most certainly have some of the answers, too. Only by trying our best both collectively and individually to make sense of where we are and where we've been, only then will we take our worldwide magickal society to greater heights where truly bold, miraculous, magick is a matter of course and a way of life. By examining together a compendium of magickal techniques from around the world and identifying the universal theories therein apparent, we can discover the secrets for unlocking the full potentials of our magick. To make it happen, there's only one thing we need to do: think.

Points to Ponder

These questions are included to help inspire new ideas that extend beyond the scope of each chapter. Come up with your best answers, then revisit these questions when you finish reading the book. It's interesting to see which of our answers evolve, and which ones stay the same.

- Do you see magick in any everyday, commonplace activities or in any aspects or elements of mainstream society?

- What *is* magick exactly, to you? What defines it as such?

- What do you feel is the best way humankind can "make good" on the gift of magick?

- In what ways can learning the magickal methods of others benefit your own practice?

- Have you ever noticed any commonalities in the methods and beliefs displayed in the wide variety of magickal practices employed throughout the world? Do you have any hunches regarding such "universal principles" of magick?

one

No-Tools Body Magick

Much magick is accomplished with the mind alone. Emotionally charged thoughts—our intentions unleashed with will, carried by love in the pursuit of our ever-rising destinies: at its heart, this is what magick truly is. Successful spellcasting is not so much in the wave of the wand as it is in the mental process of the magick worker, the internal component of the spell that doesn't require special stones, candles, or other tools and trappings in order to operate. If there's a malfunction of the internal no-tools component, the magick as a whole will fail, regardless of the quality of herbs, crystals, wands, and other elements that might also be employed. Basically, if you can't make magick *without* tools, you can't make magick *with* tools, either. This might sound like a basic concept—and it is, on the surface. When we dig deeper, however, and get to the core truths of simplistic, no-tools magick, we find that herein lies the solution to many of our magickal shortcomings. By mastering and remastering the basics, we come to understand (or in many cases, simply remember!) the scope of our powers and abilities, and we gain a sense of magickal independence and skill that doesn't rely on any special preparations or extras. This liberation makes possible more spontaneous and more frequent spellcasting, which has the potential to make our world a better, more conscious, more aware, and more peaceful place.

While the tools and trappings of magick have specific applications that can be very effective, it's important to understand that what makes these magickal accessories work can be accessed at any time and requires no special equipment to "make it go." Ever heard of the "web of life" concept? This is the philosophy of all things everywhere being interconnected, linked through a common thread that courses throughout the wide, wild world. This "web" is the magickal circuitry on which our spells travel, the link that enables us to act in the here and now in a way that affects the there and later, and all magick relies on it. In order for a spell to work, the witch must be able to find and willing to travel the road between how things are and how she wants them to be. By forging and utilizing associations, making connections between ideas and energies, we are able to manipulate reality and bend it more in line with our will.

Understanding exactly what it takes to work magick with just the body, mind, and soul and mastering these essentials builds our abilities to design and cast spells that do what they're intended to do, with or without any herbs, stones, candles, or other extras. In this chapter, we'll explore some ways to make magickal connections using nothing but yourself alone.

No-Tools Body Magick Around the World

Both intentional and accidental spellcasters around the world have carried out magick with the very simplest of actions: a word, a thought, a glance, a slight yet deliberate motion. Magick cast without tools or props can indeed have profound effects and be just as powerful as a complex spell requiring multiple tools and rare ingredients. Here are some examples of how the magickal process is carried out by different practitioners around the globe, without wands, without potions, without anything at all except a body with feelings, ideas, and intentions.

It's All in the Eyes

The notorious "evil eye" is perhaps one of the most widespread and well-known examples of no-tools body magick. Evil or ill intentions are literally cast through a single look, causing hardship and sickness to the one inflicted. A belief in the evil eye is common in cultures throughout the Middle East, West Africa, parts of Asia, Central America, Mexico, the US, and Europe.

The *Æthiopica*, a Greek literary work dating from the third century CE, makes reference to the evil eye and does well to describe the manner in which the evil eye operates. Attributed to Heliodorus, the *Æthiopica* is a work of fiction, an early example of the adventure novel that nevertheless conveys some of the truths and popular perceptions of the day. The passage that follows is a conversation about a girl afflicted with the evil eye:

> *"Tell me, my good Calasiris, what is the malady that has attacked your daughter?"*
>
> *"You ought not to be surprised," I replied, "if at the time when she was heading the procession in the sight of so vast an assemblage of people, she had drawn upon herself some envious eye."*
>
> *Whereupon, smiling ironically, "Do you then," asked he, "like the vulgar in general, believe in the reality of such fascination?"*
>
> *"As much as I do in any other fact," I replied, "and the thing is this: the air which surrounds us passing through the eyes, as it were through a strainer, and also through the mouth, the teeth and the other passages, into the inward parts, whilst its external properties make their way in together with it—whatever be its quality as it flows in, of the same nature is the effect it disseminates in the recipient, so that when any one looks upon beauty with envy, he fills the circumambient air with a malignant property, and diffuses upon his neighbour the breath issuing from himself, all impregnated with bitterness, and this, being as it is of a most subtile nature, penetrates through into the very bone and marrow.*

Hence envy has frequently turned itself into a regular disease, and has received the distinctive appellation of fascination." [5]

This example conveys the notion that the evil eye is cast through envy, a belief common in many places where "the Eye" is feared. We also see here implied that the evil eye can be cast accidentally. The scene of the crime is described in a benign way that seems to indicate that such envious feelings, and the evil eye curse that often results, were a known risk and par for the course when a lady of such beauty parades her attractive personage in front of a large gathering. The crowd can't help but be envious, and even though they're not intending to harm or hex the girl, the simple expedient of emotionally charged energy poured forth from the eyes is enough to make the magick.

Many people in modern Greece still believe in the evil eye, and it's considered capable of causing issues for both human and non-human alike. People affected by the eye report depression, weakness, sleeplessness, feverishness, headaches, and nausea, while afflicted animals may experience lethargy or infertility. The evil eye is believed capable also of causing crops to fail and machinery to break down. [6]

In the Americas also, the evil eye was (and still is) very well-known, believed capable of causing injury to both physical form and spiritual body. Along the Rio Grande, a belief in the evil eye was so prevalent that a method for preventing its common spread was devised. A 1923 study of Mexican-Americans in Texas describes a practice used to stop one's self from inadvertently casting the curse:

---

5   Heliodorus, *Æthiopica*, translated passage from Charles William King, *The Gnostics and Their Remains* (London: David Nutt, 1887), 195, accessed February 1, 2012, http://www.sacred-texts.com/gno/gar/gar29.htm.

6   Richard P. H. Greenfield, "Evil Eye," in *Encyclopedia of Ancient Greece*, ed. By Nigel Wilson (New York: Routledge, 2006), 284–285.

It is claimed that the human eye has a magic power over persons or things, and the person exercising this power is said to make Ojo (Eye). Upon seeing a person or thing and admiring that person or thing, one must touch what he has seen and admired, else the person seen will become sick or the object will break. According to the belief, every one is possessed of the power to 'make Ojo.'[7]

We see here again the idea that a curse can be cast through a look alone. By a simple projection of feeling, a single blast of emotion sent out through the eyes, a magickal change is affected. What's more, there are hints here also, as in our example from the Greek *Æthiopica*, that this magick doesn't even require intention on the part of the spellcaster—everyone can make *el ojo*, and a simple oversight of failing to make physical contact with an admired object or person is enough to set the charm into action. What we can gather from all this is that our eyes are indeed powerful vehicles for delivering magick.

While you probably don't want to go around cursing folks left and right, the eyes have other magickal applications that are much less sinister. If a person can cast an "evil eye," for instance, it only follows that a "good eye" can likewise be cast. Allow awareness of your eyes as powerful spellcasting tools to bring more intention and opportunity into your daily dealings.

Just Say the Word

In addition to magick that's cast through the eyes, there's also a whole class of magick spells that are cast solely through the power of speech and sound. The human voice resonates with energetic vibrations, sound waves that travel from the mouth to the universe at large, bearing with them the magickal

---

7   Florence Johnson Scott, "Customs and Superstitions Among Texas Mexicans on the Rio Grande Border," in *Coffee in the Gourd*, ed. J. Frank Dobie (Austin, TX: Texas Folklore Society, 1923), section IV, Omens and Superstitions, accessed February 1, 2012, http://www.sacred-texts.com/ame/cig/cig14.htm.

intentions and charged emotions of the speaker. Francis Barrett, in his 1801 work *The Magus*, comments on the connection between magick and words:

> *Almost all charms are impotent without words, because words are the speech of the speaker, and the image of the thing signified or spoken of; therefore, whatever wonderful effect is intended, let the same be performed with the addition of words significative of the will or desire of the operator; for words are a kind of occult vehicle of the image conceived or begotten, and sent out of the body by the soul; therefore, all the forcible power of the spirit ought to be breathed out with vehemency, and an arduous and intent desire…* [8]

We see in this explanation an assertion that words are nearly as powerful as the intention that comes with them. Words are simply our way of expressing those internal thoughts and images we conjure in the course of our magick, and whether whispered, signed, or yelled out loud, those words are quite potent.

In Slavic cultures, magicians found that words were strong enough vehicles for spellwork to stand on their own without any accompanying rites or rituals. These word charms, called *zagovórui*, were to be spoken out loud or sung. They were considered powerful in their own rite, and no additional ceremony was required to activate them. A collection of Slavic folklore published in 1872 explains:

> *After the old prayers had passed into spells, their magical properties were often supposed to be automatic, no longer depending on the aid of the divinities they invoked, but acting, for good or for evil, by the force of their own inherent attributes.*

---

8   Francis Barrett, *The Magus* (London: Lackington, Alley and Co., 1801), 31, accessed August 1, 2012, http://www.sacred-texts.com/grim/magus /ma108.htm.

Zagovórui of this nature generally end with the phrase, "My word is firm!" or "My word will not pass away for ever!" or,—

"May my words be sticky and tough, firmer than stone, stickier than glue or resin, salter than salt, sharper than a self-cutting sword, tougher than steel. What is meant, that shall be fulfilled!" [9]

The operating force behind the *zagovórui* is in the "inherent attributes" of the chosen words, and in the firm expression of will that is also employed. How similar is the Slavic exertion of will, "What is meant, that shall be fulfilled," to the modern Wiccan "So mote it be!"

In Slavic lands, it was well understood that the power of words indeed runs deep. An old proverb warns of the unstoppable force of the spoken word:

Among the old Slavonians, as among all other peoples, spoken words were supposed to possess certain magical powers. In their figurative language the lips and the teeth are often spoken of as locks, of which the key is the tongue. When that has once unloosened them, out shoots the word, like an arrow from a bow, and it is capable of flying straight to, and acting directly upon, the object at which it is aimed by its utterer. "A word is not a sparrow," says a Russian proverb; "once you let it fly out, you will never catch it again." [10]

We can see here how the power of words is linked to their use as symbols for what those words represent: the lips and teeth are the locks, the key is the tongue, and the unleashed words themselves possess "certain magical powers" that can hit a target as sure as an arrow. There is magickal power in such figurative language, as it forges a link between object-at-hand and all

9   W. E. S. Ralston, MA, *Songs of the Russian People* (London: Ellis and Green, 1872), 365, accessed May 7, 2012, http://www.sacred-texts.com /neu/srp/srp11.htm.

10   *Ibid.*, 358–359.

that it symbolizes, connecting the magician to additional sources of energy that can help along the spellcasting.

In Italy also was the symbolic strength of a word enough to unlock its magick. It was believed that a certain animal horn offered a cure from the evil eye, and over time the mere saying of the word for horn came to suffice to ward off the malady. So too does uttering the word for "garlic" in Greece do the trick, as garlic is a remedy for envious types of speech and other breaches that can inflict others with the evil eye. In Arabic lands, shouting the word for iron was enough to repel the evil jinn, a class of mythical, malicious demons.[11] We might surmise that one easy way to craft a word charm is to simply choose a word that symbolizes the power you want to invoke. For example, a simple spell for protection might be the name of a protective goddess, or the single word "safety."

Word charms are used around the world for every purpose from breaking a curse to healing a wound. One North-Germanic spoken spell for healing is powerful enough to take the "heat" out of scalds and burns. Though originating in Germany, the charm has been a part of American folk magick traditions for quite some time. I first learned it from my mom, who learned it from her grandmother. Though Christianized, the charm shows its Pagan roots in the mention of the "three angels," thought to refer to the early Germanic belief in the "three maidens" who dwell in green places gathering healing herbs and flowers:

There were three angels came from East and West—
One brought fire and another brought frost,
And the third it was the Holy Ghost,

---

11   Robert Means Lawerence, *The Magic of the Horse-Shoe With Other Folk-Lore Note* (Cambridge: The Riverside Press, 1898), chapter VI, Iron as a Protective Charm, accessed August 1, 2012, http://www.sacred-texts.com /etc/mhs/mhs09.htm.

Out fire, in frost, in the Name
of the Father, Son, and Holy Ghost. [12]

We find here a harmonious blending of beliefs, and an excellent example of how word charms can be personalized to suit our own perspectives and understanding. While folk magick is widely practiced, many who do so, living in Christian communities where magick is considered the Devil's work, don't choose to think of it that way. This example illustrates how easily a spell can be disguised as a Christian prayer, though the expression of magickal intention and the application of magickal method remains quite clear.

Although the words used for making magick and the methods of saying those words differs from place to place around the world, one commonality seems to be the belief in the necessity of intention. Merely uttering a magick word or words is not enough to make magick; it's the spellcaster's *intention*, their awareness of the word being a power word that forges the connection that makes the magick possible. Whether it's an Arabic spell for protection or a North-Germanic healing charm, the words are spoken with the conscious knowledge that those words will have a magickal effect.

Another point common to much magick expressed through the voice is that the word charms tend to be repetitive, with certain words or phrases being uttered more than once, or in the case of single-word charms, repeating the charm a certain number of times. Alliteration, or staff-rhyme, is also common. Not all word charms contain these examples, of course, but enough of them do that the similarities are worth noting. Let's take a look at a few more specific examples of word charms from around the world to illustrate these commonalities:

---

12   Edward Clodd, *Tom Tit Tot* (London: Duckworth, and Co., 1898), "Words of Power," accessed March 23, 2013, http://www.sacred-texts .com/neu/celt/ttt/ttt11.htm.

Malay Jampis

Malaysian magickal practitioners use many spoken charms, called "*jampis*" or "*do'as*." Although rituals often accompany the charms, they are also sometimes used on their own without any extra tools or ceremony. In *Shaman, Saiva, and Sufi: A Study of the Evolution of Malay Magic* by R. O. Winstedt, the author offers an example of a Malay spoken charm used to thwart one's enemies:

> *Om! King of genies!*
> *The rock-splitting lightning is my voice!*
> *Michael is with me!*
> *In virtue of my use of this charm*
> *To make heavy and lock,*
> *I lock the hearts of all my adversaries,*
> *I make dumb their tongues,*
> *I lock their mouths,*
> *I tie their hands,*
> *I fetter their feet.*
> *Not till rock moves*
> *Shall their hearts be moved;*
> *Not till earth my mother moves*
> *Shall their hearts be moved.*[13]

In the line, "The rock-splitting lightning is my voice," we see the clear intention and consciousness of the Malay magician. By equating the voice to "rock-splitting lightning," the Malay expresses the necessary belief that the words will indeed have power and effect. Further, we see the repetition so often present in spoken charms: the word for "lock" is used three times, while the phrase for "shall their hearts be moved" is included twice. We see also repetition in the lines:

---

13   R. O. Winstedt, *Shaman, Saiva, and Sufi: A Study of the Evolution of Malay Magic* (Glasgow: The University Press, 1925), chapter IV, The Malay Charm, accessed March 9, 2012, http://www.sacred-texts.com/sha/sss /sss06.htm.

I lock the hearts of all my adversaries,
I make dumb their tongues,
I lock their mouths,
I tie their hands,
I fetter their feet.

Here, we have the personal pronoun repeated several times, coupled with similar, somewhat repetitive intentions. The repetition creates a rising, building power throughout the course of the word charm, and also ensures a thorough binding of the adversaries in question.

Hindu Hymns and Mantras

In the hymns and mantras of Hindu culture, we also find repetition as well as the application of intention. The *Atharvaveda*, an important Hindu sacred text, contains many word charms. One charm meant to work instantly in the moment to stop the flow of blood from an open wound is rather similar to the North-Germanic word charm to take away the immediate pain of a burn:

The maidens that go yonder, the veins, clothed in red garments, like sisters without a brother, bereft of strength, they shall stand still!

Stand still, thou lower one, stand still, thou higher one; do thou in the middle also stand still! The most tiny (vein) stands still: may then the great artery also stand still! Of the hundred arteries, and the thousand veins, those in the middle here have indeed stood still. At the same time the ends have ceased (to flow).

Around you has passed a great sandy dike: stand ye still, pray take your case! [14]

---

14   Maurice Bloomfield, *Hymns of the Atharva-Veda: Sacred Books of the East, Vol. 42* (Oxford, UK: Oxford University Press, 1897), I, 17, Charm to Stop the Flow of Blood, accessed March 28, 2012, http://www.sacred-texts.com /hin/sbe42/av034.htm.

In the lines "bereft of strength," "they shall stand still" (and variations), "the ends have ceased to flow," and "Around you has passed a great sandy dike: stand ye still, pray take your case!" is revealed the necessary intention and belief in the charm's power. By saying it's so, it becomes so. Like other word charms, this formula operates primarily through the conscious use of the will projected through the utterance of words. We also see in this example repetition, with variations on the words, "stand still" repeated no less than eight times!

Scottish Folk Charms

In the *Carmina Gadelica*, a compilation of charms, hymns, and incantations collected from the oral folk traditions of Scotland originally published in 1900, we find a word charm for counteracting the evil eye, translated from the Gaelic into English by Alexander Carmicheal:

> *THE fair spell that lovely Mary sent,*
> *Over stream, over sea, over land,*
> *Against incantations, against withering glance,*
> *Against inimical power,*
> *Against the teeth of wolf,*
> *Against the testicles of wolf,*
> *Against the three crooked cranes,*
> *Against the three crooked bones,*
>
> *...*
>
> *Whoso made to thee the eye,*
> *May it lie upon himself,*
> *May it lie upon his house,*
> *May it lie upon his flocks,*
> *May it lie upon his substance,*
> *May it lie upon his fatness,*
> *May it lie upon his means,*
> *May it lie upon his children,*

May it lie upon his wife,
May it lie upon his descendants.
I will subdue the eye,
I will suppress the eye,
And I will banish the eye,

…

Three lovely little maidens,
Born the same night with Christ,
If alive be these three to-night,
Life be a near thee, poor beast.[15]

Here again is the repetition common to so many of our spoken magickal charms. First, we have repetition in the stating of the ills this charm can prevent: "Against incantations," "against withering glance," etc. Then, we have further repetition as the curse is reversed: "May it lie upon himself," "May it lie upon his house," "May it lie upon his flocks," and so on.

Another interesting element to note is the mention here of the "three lovely little maidens" juxtaposed with the mentions of Mary and Christ. Much like our example of the Christianized but still overtly Pagan North-Germanic word charm for counteracting burns, this present sample reflects the blending of Christianity into the Pagan folk magick and customs of the Scottish people. We can guess that the charm has probably changed somewhat from its original form, and from this likelihood we might assume that the elements essential to the proper construction of a word charm were carefully left intact as alterations and additions were made.

---

15   Alexander Carmichael, *Carmina Gadelica: Hymns and Incantations, Volume 2* (Edinburgh, UK: T. and A. Constable, 1900), 53, accessed June 4, 2012, http://www.sacred-texts.com/neu/celt/cg2025.htm.

Slavic Zagovors

In the Slavic *zagovors* already mentioned, we frequently see the same commonalities of repetition and intention. Here's another example from Ralston's *Songs of the Russian People* that does well to highlight these features:

> *I, the servant of God ————, stand still, uttering a blessing.*
> *I, crossing myself, go from the room to the door, from the courtyard to the gates.*
>
> *I go out into the open field, to the eastern side. On the eastern side stands an izbá [cottage or room], in the middle of the izbá lies a plank, under the plank is the LONGING.*
>
> *The Longing weeps, the Longing sobs, waiting to get at the white light. The white light, the fair sun, waits, enjoys itself, and rejoices.*
>
> *So may He wait longing to get to me, and [having done so] may he enjoy himself and rejoice! And without me let it not be possible for him to live, nor to be, nor to eat, nor to drink; neither by the morning dawn, nor by the evening glow.*
>
> *As a fish without water, as a babe without its mother, without its mother's milk, cannot live, so may he, without me, not be able to live, nor to be, nor to eat, nor to drink; neither by the morning dawn, nor by the evening glow; neither every day, not at mid-day, nor under the many stars, nor together with the stormy winds. Neither under the sun by day, nor under the moon by night.*
>
> *Plunge thyself, O longing I gnaw thy way, O longing, into his breast, into his heart; grow and increase in all his veins, in all his bones, with pain and thirst for me!* [16]

The assertion of the spellcaster being a "servant of god" who is "uttering a blessing" provides the necessary belief in the power of the magick, and the

---

16   W. E. S. Ralston, MA, *Songs of the Russian People* (London: Ellis and Green, 1872), 369, accessed May 7, 2012, http://www.sacred-texts.com /neu/srp/srp11.htm.

confidence and intention of the petitioner is further expressed in the line "O longing I gnaw thy way." Repetition here comes in the lines asserting that it will not be possible for the target of the spell to "live, nor to be, nor to eat, nor to drink; neither by the morning dawn, nor by the evening glow."

This charm also shares another point common to many word charms—the build-up. We have in the second repetition an extension: "…neither by the morning dawn, nor by the evening glow; neither every day, not at mid-day, nor under the many stars, nor together with the stormy winds. Neither under the sun by day, nor under the moon by night," while the first repetition of the phrase ends after "evening glow." With each additional command, the energy rises and the charm is fortified and "set," just as a bit of magick might depend on a build-up and release of energy when casting a spell using tools other than words.

Magick in Movement

Sometimes a mere movement or action is enough to cast a charm. The Irish Druids, for instance, had a method of detecting deception or expelling evil through a simple motion of the thumb. James Bonwick writes of the practice in his 1894 work *Irish Druids and Old Irish Religions*, referencing a legend surrounding the hero Fionn:

> … the chewing of one's thumb was sometimes as effectual a disenchanter as the elevation or marking of the cross in subsequent centuries. Thus, when Fionn was once invited to take a seat beside a fair lady on her way to a palace, he, having some suspicion, put his thumb between his teeth, and she immediately changed into an ugly old hag with evil in her heart. That was a simple mode of detection, but may have been efficacious only in the case of such a hero as Fionn. Certainly, many a bad spirit would be expelled, in a rising quarrel, if one party were wise enough to put his thumb between his teeth.[17]

---

17   James Bonwick, *Irish Druids and Old Irish Religions* (London: Griffith, Farran, 1894), 50, accessed June 5, 2012, http://www.sacred-texts.com /pag/idr/idr12.htm.

In the same work, Bonwick offers another rather unusual example of body movement magick performed by the Irish:

The poet chews a piece of the flesh of a red pig, or of a dog or cat, and brings it afterwards on a flag behind the door, and chants an incantation upon it, and offers it to idol gods; and his idol gods are brought to him, but he finds them not on the morrow. And he pronounces incantations on his two palms; and his idol gods are also brought to him, in order that his sleep may not be interrupted. And he lays his two palms on his two cheeks, and thus falls asleep. And he is watched in order that no one may disturb or interrupt him, until everything about which he is engaged is revealed to him, which may be a minute, or two, or three, or as long as the ceremony requires—one palm over the other across his cheeks.[18]

Though we see in this example the use of flesh and idols, these are but an accompaniment to the heart of the ritual, intended to help assure the magicians uninterrupted sleep while the primary magical work is completed. The core of the magick, the connection forged between this realm and the other, is ultimately brought about not through pig's flesh or idols, but through the prophetic and mystical sleep manifested by the simple yet odd positioning of enchanted palms upon the face of the dreamer.

Body movement magick was practiced in ancient Egypt, as well. A text found on the east wall of the antechamber of the Pyramid of Unas, a structure that was built around 2375 BCE during Egypt's Fifth Dynasty, offers this charm for deterring robbers:

Utterance 283.
Indeed I dart this left thumb-nail of mine against you, I strike a

---

18   James Bonwick, *Irish Druids and Old Irish Religions* (London: Griffith, Farran, 1894), 61, accessed June 5, 2012, http://www.sacred-texts.com/pag/idr/idr12.htm.

*blow with it on behalf of Min and the ikiw. O you, who are wont
to rob, do not rob.*[19]

Here, the simple act of making a jabbing motion with the left thumb-nail is enough to call down the wrath of the great sky god Min, a sufficient threat for deterring potential thieves.

What stands out about the body magick of the Druids and the Egyptians is their oddness—we wouldn't typically bite our thumb or jab at the air with it; sleeping with our palms on our cheeks is far out of the ordinary. It's in the bizarreness of these magickal motions that their power resides.

Magickal movement doesn't always have an odd or peculiar quality, though. Sometimes, the actions are very straightforward. Throughout Europe, for instance, mimetic motion was widely used to achieve corresponding magickal goals. In *Ancient Art and Ritual*, Jane Harrison highlights some of the most common practices:

> *In Swabia and among the Transylvanian Saxons it is a common
> custom … for a man who has some hemp to leap high in the field
> in the belief that this will make the hemp grow tall. In many parts
> of Germany and Austria the peasant thinks he can make the flax
> grow tall by dancing or leaping high or by jumping backwards
> from a table; the higher the leap the taller will be the flax that
> year … In some parts of Eastern Russia the girls dance one by one
> in a large hoop at midnight on Shrove Tuesday. The hoop is decked
> with leaves, flowers and ribbons, and attached to it are a small
> bell and some flax. While dancing within the hoop each girl has to
> wave her arms vigorously and cry, "Flax, grow," or words to that
> effect. When she has done she leaps out of the hoop or is lifted out
> of it by her partner.*[20]

---

19   R. O. Faulkner, *The Ancient Egyptian Pyramid Texts* (1969; repr., Stilwell: Digireads.com, 2007), 86.

20   Jane Harrison, *Ancient Art and Ritual* (London: Thornton Butterworth Ltd, 1913), 31–32, accessed March 3, 2012, http://www.sacred-texts.com /cla/aar/aar04.htm.

Whether leaping high or dancing wildly, the movement of the people instructs the earth to respond in kind, and through these simple imitative actions, crops were made to grow. A high leap equals tall hemp; an energetic dance makes for vivacious flax plants. The magician has only to imitate through body movement the desired outcome, and a powerful spell is cast.

The Hindu *mudras* are another example of body magick worth noting. Mudras are specific hand shapes and body postures used in Hindu religion and yogic practice to intentionally control and activate the flow of energy throughout the body. Mudras can involve just the hands or the entire body, and they're typically used alongside conscious breathing techniques. It's believed that making a mudra makes connections in the energetic circuitry or channels within our bodies, an effect that can be used for achieving healing, greater energy, trance states, and more.

One mudra is called the *prana mudra*, formed by touching the tips of the pinkies and ring fingers to the thumbs. The prana mudra is believed to activate life energy and improve overall health and vitality. In *The Healing Power of Mudras*, Rajendar Menen cites an increase in the life force, improved vision, improved circulation, and better immune function among the benefits of activating the prana mudra. [21]

While the magick of movement can operate on a variety of principles, be it through oddity, mimicry, or conscious design, one thing common to all these techniques is the ingredient of intent. The magician *knows* that their movements and body positions will have a specific effect, and in this belief, the magick is wrought and the spell is cast.

Common Threads and New Perspectives

In this chapter, we've explored many means for making magick without herbs, stones, elaborate rituals, or other aids. You know the power of will, the power of intention, and the power of our own bodies can be used to

---

21   Rajendar Menen, *The Healing Power of Mudras* (New Delhi: V & S Publishers, 2011), 12.

cast effective magick without a single tool or prop. You know that the eyes are an effective instrument of magick, able to project emotionally charged thoughts capable of affecting humans, animals, crops, and even machinery, with or without the conscious intention of the spellcaster. You've seen how magicians around the world have used their own voices to cast magick to deter enemies, heal burns, stop bleeding, and more, and you know that word charms operate primarily through the projection of will. You know also that intention is required to transform the voice into a tool for magick, and you're familiar with several techniques for making word charms more powerful, be it through figurative language, repetition, alliteration, or a build-up of energy. You're familiar with many different ways magick workers have used movement to achieve their spellcasting ends, and you understand how the magick of motion might be based on oddity, mimicry, or conscious design.

Magick is a personal art, functioning ultimately through no greater medium than the person who casts it. Whether our spells are very complex, involving lots of tools and trappings, or really quite simple, cast with nothing more than the self alone, the more we put into our magick energetically, the greater the effect that results. Get to know the power of your own body, and discover how mastering no-tools magick can make your spellwork more precise, more effective, more spontaneous, and more integral to your daily life as a witch.

No-Tools Magick Spells

When you're used to working magick with tools and other trappings, casting a simple spell using the mind and body alone can seem a bit bland—that is, until you *really* try it! Focus on precisely executing each step in the process (however brief); make each thought, each word, each movement count. Here are a few exercises in no-tools magick to try. If you're a practicing witch, most likely you have performed similar magick countless times. This time, however, pay careful attention to everything going on within, *and as a result of,* each step of the magick.

Casting the Good Eye

The Good Eye is the opposite of the Evil Eye—instead of causing misfortune, the Good Eye sends to the receiver a feeling of love and compassion. To cast the Good Eye on a friend, foe, or stranger, try this. Open your eyes wide and think of a cool air flowing through your irises. Conjure a vision of light and a feeling of love in your heart, and project this energy out through your eyes as you gaze upon the one you wish to thus bless, just as you would send energy out of your fingertips or through a wand. Eye contact is essential; don't break it while casting the charm. Like the Evil Eye, the Good Eye is cast in a matter of seconds and typically sets to work straight away. The eyes are powerful vehicles for conveying magickal energy, and aren't limited to the specific applications here discussed. For variation, try developing techniques for casting the Prosperous Eye, the Chill Out Eye, and other unique innovations of your very own.

Your Own Words of Power

Need a boost of luck to get that new job, or could you use some extra protection against that gossipy neighbor? Why not create your own simple word charm just right for the situation at hand? Your word charm could be a song, a mantra, a poem, a chant. Perhaps a one-word charm suits you best. Experiment, and go with what feels right. We tend to put much stock in the formulas of magicians past without realizing that someone just like us, somewhere along the line, created these magickal recipes. As experienced magicians and intuitive, conscious, creative, thinking beings, our own ideas are just as valid. Let traditional elements such as intent, repetition, alliteration, the build-up, and figurative language inspire and guide you when crafting your word charm, and consider also making use of words with inherent magickal properties. Ultimately though, let your personal taste, creativity, and psychic insight have full reign. Once you've decided on a word charm, whenever you need it, simply utter the word or words out loud as you project your will and intention. If you communicate through a visual language such as American Sign Language, just move your hands with precision and deliberation as you express each portion of the magickal phrase.

Magickal Motion Charms

From waking to bedtime, take notice of how your energy flows throughout your body during your daily routine. Do any movements seem to produce energetic effects within your body that might be useful for magick? For example, might you be able to cast a spell by adding intent to your workout, to your cooking, to your kicking back and relaxing? Observe your energies while engaging in various movements, various postures, hand positions, etc. Try jumping, laying down, dancing, or sitting in a meditative pose. Perform odd motions, and pretend like you're carrying out various actions, from flying an airplane to opening a locked door. Make a note of anything that strikes you, then try some experimental movement charms to test your discoveries. For instance, if you notice you feel a little more cheerful anytime you raise your fingertips above your head, try using the motion as a charm to consciously bring joy into your spirit whenever you're feeling low.

Points to Ponder

- Do you feel that ritual tools such as wands, candles, bells, and pentacles are necessary for successful spellwork? Why or why not?

- Do you think humanity's earliest experiences with magick may have been with no-tools body magick, spells cast through eyes, movements, or words alone? Do you think magickal tools have been in use from the very beginning? How has the invention or discovery of magickal tools helped the spellcaster?

- Does knowing how to cast magick without tools offer advantages? What are some situations in which no-tools body magick could come in handy?

- In addition to body movements and magick cast through the eyes as well as words, what other forms of no-tools magick can you think of?

- Magickal tools aren't necessary but they're useful, and we like them. What is it that these tools do exactly to enhance the spellcasting process? For what shortcomings can they compensate? For what shortcomings can they *not* compensate?

- Can you think of some ways to conveniently incorporate no-tools body magick into your daily routine? What benefits might you gain? Could mastering magick *without* tools improve your ability to cast magick *with* tools?

two

Potion Making and Mixing Magick

We fill the cauldron with fresh water and place in it a delicate jasmine blossom. We light the candles and call on the Goddess. We stand beneath the streaming moonlight and we allow the energies flowing around us to swirl within us and into the substance of the brew, combining all these disparate energies and essences together with the power of our consciousness, will, and intent. In magick, we mix—taking a bit of energy here, and mixing it with a bit of energy there, creating our own recipes for realities we wish to manifest. By mastering some techniques that can be used for mixing and combining energies, the witch gains a versatile tool that can be employed for magickal purposes in virtually any situation, from increasing one's strength to fostering cooperation between individuals. In this chapter, we'll look at some of the ways that potion making and other forms of mixing magick have been employed throughout the world, then we'll use this knowledge to craft effective modern methods just right for today.

Potion Making and Mixing
Magick Around the World

Magick to combine energies can be carried out in countless ways, of course, from imitative magick to various types of binding spells. One of the most widespread ways of magickally mixing energies, however, goes in the mouth. Throughout the world, magickal practitioners have found that food and drink provide excellent media for combining and mixing energies. In the act of mixing a drinkable potion or food item, the energies of ingredients (intentionally selected for their attributes) are combined into a magickal mixture with a unified purpose. Once ingested, the energies of the mixture combine with the energies of the person ingesting it, infusing the individual with the desired essence or attribute.

The Zulu are among the many peoples who have combined magickal energies with their own through the acts of eating or drinking. Numbering around 11 to 12 million, the Zulu are the largest ethnic group in South Africa. Although today the population is largely Christianized, ancient traditions of magickal practice remain. Among these ancient traditions, the use of herbal mixtures for mystical and medicinal purposes is among the most prevalent in modern times, and herbalist healers known as *inyangas* are still widely sought after. The inyangas use a combination of information obtained from ancestors via divination, and their own knowledge and experience of plants, minerals, and other ingredients, to craft their medicinal blends. These medicines, called *muthi* or *muti*, are often administered orally. It's believed that the effects of the muthi can be absorbed into the body through contact with the mouth, skin, nasal passages, and other points of entry. Although the medicines are meant to cure physical ailments, they have a spiritual component as well, capable of healing injuries to the soul such as might be incurred through an attack of malicious witchcraft. The Zulu distinguish between the use of *umuthi omhlope*—medicinal potions for positive intentions like healing, and the use of *umuthi omnyama*—magickal mixtures designed to cause death, sickness, or other types of negative effects. [22]

The Zulu have a long history of using muthi and other edible magickal mixtures to affect both the physical body and the spirit. In *The Religious System of the Amazulu*, an 1870 work by Henry Callaway, another traditional act of mixing magick is mentioned. Callaway describes the ritualistic consumption of meat covered with *umsizi*,[23] a black mixture consisting of a combination of charred and powdered plant and animal matter:

> For on the day the army is summoned and assembles at the chief's, the chief slaughters cattle, and they are then skinned; the first meat they eat is black, being always smeared with umsizi. All eat the meat, each a slice, that they may be brave, and not fearful. [24]

In smearing the magickal mixture directly onto the foodstuffs, the Zulu were able to successfully combine the energies of the food with the powerful vibrations of the sacred *umsizi*.

The Zulu used different magickal potion and powder recipes for different purposes, custom blended to suit the needs of unique individuals and situations. Ingredients might be chosen for their physical effects or for their mystical symbolism. In certain recipes, for instance, parts of lions, jackals, or other wild animals were included to promote agility, strength, or other desired traits embodied by these fearsome beasts, while other recipes

22   Adam Ashforth, *Witchcraft, Violence, and Democracy in South Africa* (Chicago: University of Chicago Press, 2005), 52–57, 133–142.

23   The word *umsizi* is also used to denote a disease caused by a mixture of witchcraft and infidelity, in addition to its meaning as a magickal powder or medicine here described.

24   Henry Callaway, *The Religious System of the Amazulu* (Springvale, Natal: J. A. Blair, 1870), 443, accessed January 15, 2012, http://www.sacred-texts.com/afr/rsa/rsa11.htm.

call for herbs with known psychoactive or medicinal properties.[25] In our present example, when the food is eaten, the people become "brave, and not fearful," having absorbed the magickal essence of the enchanted food and thus combined the bravery and courage there encased with their own essence. The spirit of the person eating is infused with the spirit of the food, which has been infused with the spirit of the plants or animals from which it is made and charmed.

Jewish magicians also combined and mixed magickal energies through the acts of eating or drinking. In Joshua Trachtenberg's *Jewish Magic and Superstition*, the author writes of the use of food as a medium for administering magick:

> *This means of applying magic is best exemplified in the field of medicine, where the spells or the mystical names were frequently consumed just as though they were so many cathartics to expel the disease-demons. The same procedure was favored in charms to obtain understanding and wisdom, and to sharpen the memory. The injunction is frequently encountered to write the names, or the Biblical verses, or the spell upon a cake (the preparation of which was often quite elaborate), or upon a hard-boiled egg that had been shelled, and to devour it… Magic cakes were also prepared for a bride to ensure fecundity, and were administered on various occasions for good luck.* [26]

This example reveals a belief that healing energies as well as wisdom and mental acuity can be absorbed through the act of eating something infused with the desired energy. We see also that one straightforward way to

25   Amazulu: The Life of the Zulu Nation, "Zulu Healing," accessed March 24, 2013, http://library.thinkquest.org/27209/Healing.htm.

26   Joshua Trachtenberg, *Jewish Magic and Superstition* (New York: Behrman's Jewish Book House, 1939), 122–123, accessed January 11, 2012, http://www.sacred-texts.com/jud/jms/jms11.htm.

empower foodstuffs for this purpose is to simply write upon it your intent or perhaps another word charm or symbol that appropriately conveys your magickal wish.

Trachtenberg offers us further details about Jewish procedures for potion-making:

> To gain understanding it was enough to recite a group of seven names seven times over a cup of old wine and drink it, though usually the procedure was more naïve. Some prescriptions required that the spell be written on leaves or bits of paper and then soaked in wine or water, or that it be written with honey on the inside of a cup and then dissolved in water, and the resulting decoction swallowed. This was the essential character of the love-potions that were so popular during the Middle Ages; however fantastic their ingredients, their purpose was to transmit the charm in physical form to the body of the desired one. [27]

Intention, we might infer, can be transmitted to and combined with the energies of a liquid to form a potion by the expedients of the human voice or the written word. We can assume the first technique in this example works by combining the vibrations of the human voice and the energies therein expressed with the energies of the wine, and then combining the resulting concoction with the energies of the wisdom-seeker who drinks it. The other recipes mentioned in the example call for the mixing of energies to be accomplished through dissolving—the intent-infused leaves or paper scraps, the intent-infused word written with honey, dissolved and mixed into the energies of the wine or the water and thus transferred into and combined with the energies of the body into which the potion is taken.

---

27   Joshua Trachtenberg, *Jewish Magic and Superstition* (New York: Behrman's Jewish Book House, 1939), 123, accessed January 11, 2012, http://www.sacred-texts.com/jud/jms/jms11.htm.

In Polynesia as well, the practice of combining energies through consumption is well known. A legend regarding a powerful sorcerer named Kiki and a rival magician and chief named Tamure does well to illustrate:

> *As soon as they had landed, the old sorcerer called out to them that they were welcome to his village, and invited them to come up to it: so they went up to the village: and when they reached the square in the centre, they seated themselves upon the ground; and some of Kiki's people kindled fire in an enchanted oven, and began to cook food in it for the strangers. Kiki sat in this house, and Tamure on the ground just outside the entrance to it, and he there availed himself of this opportunity to repeat incantations over the threshold of the house, so that Kiki might be enchanted as he stepped over it to come out. When the food in the enchanted oven was cooked, they pulled off the coverings, and spread it out upon clean mats. The old sorcerer now made his appearance out of his house and he invited Tamure to come and eat food with him; but the food was all enchanted, and his object in asking Tamure to eat with him was, that the enchanted food might kill him ...* [28]

Here, we see that the energy of the "enchanted oven" itself is combined with the energy of the food in order to fill that food with the magickal power desired. There are apparently no herbs or other ingredients required; the curse placed on the oven is sufficient to likewise curse the food cooked within it. We might infer here that a close proximity of energies is enough to combine them. The food we might assume would operate in the typical manner, combining with the energies of the one who ingests it, which in this case, would lead to death. Luckily, the rival sorcerer Tamure isn't foolish

---

28   Sir George Grey, *Polynesian Mythology and Ancient Traditional History of the New Zealanders: As Furnished by Their Priests and Chiefs* (London: John Murray, 1855), 201–202, accessed March 23, 2013, http://www .sacred-texts.com/pac/grey/grey019htm.

enough to let his guard down, and the word magick he performs pays off. The story goes on to describe how Tamure not only enchanted the threshold of Kiki's dwelling, but also spoke magickal words as a countercharm whilst the cursed food was consumed. According to the legend, Kiki became very ill soon after his encounter with Tamure, while Tamure returned home safely.

Another rather notorious bit of mixing magick that warrants examining is the love potion. Employed throughout the world to incite obsession, interest, or undying devotion, one thing love potions *don't* seem to do is cause actual love. At worst, traditional love potions were actually poisonous, containing toxic or psychoactive ingredients such as datura, a.k.a. jimson weed, a plant in the nightshade family that causes delirium. Mandrake and henbane were other poisonous yet popular choices.[29] Sometimes, love potions weren't so much dangerously toxic as they were disgusting. Charles Godfrey Leland provides us with a sampling of unappetizing yet effective Roma recipes for love potions in his 1891 book *Gypsy Sorcery and Fortune Telling*:

> *The simplest and least hurtful beverage which they give unknown to persons to secure love is made as follows:—On any of the nights mentioned they collect in the meadows gander-goose (Romání, vast bengeszkero—devil's hand; in Latin, Orchis maculata; German, Knaberkraut), the yellow roots of which they dry and crush and mix with their menses, and this they introduce to the food of the person whose love they wish to secure...*
>
> *To the less revolting philtres belongs one in which the girl puts the ashes of a burnt piece of her dress which had been wet with perspiration and has, perhaps, hair adhering to it, into a man's food or drink.*[30]

---

29   Glen Hanson, Peter Venturelli, and Annette Fleckenstein, *Drugs and Society* (Sudbury, MA: Jones and Bartlett Publishers, LLC, 2009), 327.

30   Charles Godfrey Leland, *Gypsy Sorcery and Fortune Telling* (London: T. Fisher Unwin, 1891), 120–121, accessed January 2, 2012, http://www.sacred-texts.com/pag/gsft/gsft09.htm.

In the first formula, the energy of the magickal roots of the early purple orchid, here called gander-goose or devil's hand, combines with the energy of the woman's menses, and this combined essence, when ingested, mixes with the spirit of the desired person. In the second recipe, the woman's dress, sweat, and hair are combined with the energies of food or drink. We see in both blends that bodily-derived ingredients or other very personal items containing a person's energetic signature were deemed quite useful in the creation of a love potion. We might extend this principle and conclude that ingredients which contain the energetic essence of a thing, whether through the fact of being made of it or kept in close proximity, are powerful substances to include in potions and other forms of mixing magick. In the case of these Roma love potions, such ingredients are enough to win attention and sway affections. While love itself can't be magickally manifested, these potions were apparently enough to incite some interest!

In Papau New Guinea also, mixing magickal potions for the purpose of inducing love is a widely known practice. In a seminar given in 2006 by Steven Edmund Winduo of the University of Canterbury, the modern use of a potion to procure love is described. The Nagum Boiken he references are a coastal culture of the Prince Alexander Mountains:

> *The Nagum Boiken use A. Wilkensiana in love magic to attract a woman. The leaves are squeezed and rubbed on smoke or mixed with drink and given to the woman who is the target of a man's love magic.*[31]

The herb he refers to, *Acalypha wilkensiana*, is an evergreen shrub with known value as an anti-fungal agent.[32] Commonly called copperleaf

---

31   Steven Edmund Winduo, "Indigenous Knowledge of Medicinal Plants in Papau New Guinea" (paper presented to the Macmillan Brown Center for Pacific Studies, 2006), 15, accessed March 15, 2013, http://www.pacs. canterbury.ac.nz/documents/Steven%20Winduo%20Macmillan %20Brown%20Seminar.pdf.

32   "Acalypha," The World Botanical Associates, accessed March 3, 2013, http://www.worldbotanical.com/acalypha.htm.

and known for its vivid and colorful foliage, it's perhaps the plant's endur-ing beauty more than its medicinal properties that makes it an appealing ingredient for a love potion. In this example, we find two ways the copper-leaf's essence can be combined with an individual's essence to produce the desired magickal effect. By rubbing the plant on other herbs to be smoked and inhaled, or by mixing the plant with a liquid and drinking it, the ener-gies of the plant are effectively blended with those of the intended target of the love spell.

As wise witches know, the use of love potions shouldn't be taken lightly, as the practice does have its potential side effects and consequences. In Lady Francesca Speranza Wilde's 1887 work *Ancient Legends, Mystic Charms, and Superstitions of Ireland*, the author relates some traditional Irish wisdom regarding the love philtre:

> *Some of the country people have still a traditional remembrance of very powerful herbal remedies, and love potions are even now frequently in use. They are generally prepared by an old woman; but must be administered by the person who wishes to inspire the tender passion. At the same time, to give a love potion is considered a very awful act, as the result may be fatal, or at least full of danger.*
>
> *A fine, handsome young man, of the best character and conduct, suddenly became wild and reckless, drunken and disorderly, from the effect, it was believed, of a love potion administered to him by a young girl who was passionately in love with him. When she saw the change produced in him by her act, she became moody and nervous, as if a constant terror were over her, and no one ever saw her smile again. Finally, she became half deranged, and after a few years of a strange, solitary life, she died of melancholy and despair. This was said to be "The Love-potion Curse."* [33]

---

33   Lady Francesca Speranza Wilde, *Ancient Legends, Mystic Charms, and Superstitions of Ireland* (London: Ward & Downey, 1887), "A Love Potion," accessed March 23, 2013, http://www.sacred-texts.com/neu/celt /ali/ali104.htm.

One might suspect that the potion given to the poor young man here mentioned contained poisonous herbs or other toxic ingredients, but the spiritual warning in the story also warrants attention. If a potion is used in any way to control a loved one, that loved one will no longer act like themselves because they'll no longer *be* just themselves—combined with your own magickal will, the potential lover's spirit will be faded from the lack of freedom and diminished by the restrictions placed upon it. Be wise and think twice before using a love potion!

Potions for love and other purposes were common in Mexican culture, as well. In her essay "Customs and Superstitions among Texas Mexicans on the Rio Grande Border," Florence Johnson Scott relates a traditional potion recipe for calming the nerves. The *susto* here mentioned means literally fright, and refers to a state of nervous shock:

> *Should his malady be pronounced Susto, he must go to a graveyard and take a pinch of dust from four corners of a grave. If not near a burial place, he may, instead, go to a cross-roads and take a pinch of dust from the four corners of the highway. Then to the dust must be added a piece of red ribbon, a gold ring, and a sprig of palm leaf that has been blessed. From this mixture a tea is made and seven doses are swallowed. However, the tea has an external efficacy also. It is suddenly poured into a brass kettle that has been heated very hot. The sizzling sound made by the escaping steam gives the patient a start, and acts as a sort of antidote to the shock from which he is suffering.*[34]

---

34   Florence Johnson Scott, "Customs and Superstitions among Texas Mexicans on the Rio Grande Border," in *Coffee in the Gourd*, ed. J. Frank Dobie (Austin, TX: Texas Folklore Society, 1923), section IV, Omens and Superstitions, accessed February 1, 2012, http://www.sacred-texts.com /ame/cig/cig14.htm.

In this recipe we find that dirt taken from the four corners of a grave or a crossroads, combined with the energies of a red ribbon, a gold ring, and a blessed palm leaf creates a potion that mixes with the senses to calm the nerves and soothe shock. We might suppose that the dirt from four corners of a graveyard or crossroads supplies a grounding effect, related perhaps to the four directions, and containing also the magickal properties inherent to such locations. The goddess Mictecacihuatl, later known as Santa Muerte, is strongly associated with graveyards and is believed to watch over souls while in the depths of death, darkness, or despair, while crossroads have long corresponded to transformation, occult forces, and magick.

The inclusion of the red ribbon can probably be attributed to its Christian associations, the color red being associated with the blood of Christ and thus with the protection and salvation attributed to that godform. Red ribbons are commonly used throughout Mexico to attach *milagros* onto altars and shrines. Milagros are small metal charms symbolizing prayers or expressing gratitude, typically placed in holy places such as shrines to saints, or carried around in one's pocket for good luck and protection. The red ribbon has other symbolic possibilities, as well. In Mexican culture, the color red is associated with life, blood, passion, strength, and protection, and its usefulness in an anti-shock potion could be due in part to its correspondences with these powerful and vital energies.

The gold ring is included most likely due to the metal's inherent symbolism: fire, the sun, illumination, divinity—indeed powerful forces with which to combat fright. The palm branch has merit for its associations with spiritual victory, and like the red ribbon, it also has links with Christian symbology.

Although the choice of potion ingredients is indeed intriguing, the practical, mundane action of the brew is equally worth noting: this anti-shock tea surprises the patient back to their senses by producing a loud, sudden sizzling sound when poured into the hot brass kettle. Perhaps a modern witch might in a similar manner make use of steam, bubbles, flavors, textures, or other "surface" qualities of a potion when crafting his or her own unique magickal blends.

In addition to combining energies by ingesting foods and potions, mixing magick can be carried out through externally applied blends, as well. In Jewish magick, for instance, consuming magick cakes, eggs, and charmed drinks weren't the only ways to achieve magickal results. In *Jewish Magic and Superstition*, Joshua Trachtenberg writes:

> *Liquids that had been magically charged were also applied externally. To gain favor the suggestion was to recite various Psalms over oil and to anoint the face and hands with it… "To behold great wonders" one must bathe in scented water over which a spell has been uttered… To destroy an enemy's power one should recite given charms over wine or water and pour the liquid in front of his door… To calm a storm at sea… a mixture of rose-oil, water and salt over which the charm had been whispered, were recommended.* [35]

We here find that the power of potions can be absorbed through direct contact, be it with the skin, the bottom of a shoe, or the sea. Again we find that through the simple expedient of close proximity, energies are magickally combined. Also to note here is the use of the word *charm* to empower and activate the potion: Psalms were recited, charms were spoken or whispered, before the magickal liquids were applied.

The Roma also used their potions externally. In Charles Godfrey Leland's *Gypsy Sorcery and Fortune Telling*, the following rather curious formula for curing a livestock ailment causing external sores called *Würmer*, or "worms" is given:

---

35   Joshua Trachtenberg, *Jewish Magic and Superstition* (New York: Behrman's Jewish Book House, 1939), 123–124, accessed January 11, 2012, http://www.sacred-texts.com/jud/jms/jms11.htm.

Before sunrise wolf's milk (Wolfsmilch, rukeskro tçud) is collected, mixed with salt, garlic, and water, put into a pot, and boiled down to a brew. With a part of this the afflicted spot is rubbed, the rest is thrown into a brook, with the words:—

"Kirmora jánen ándre tçud
Andrál tçud, andré sir
Andrál sir, andré páñi,
Panensá kiyá dádeske,
Kiyá Niváseske
Pçandel tumen shelchá
Eñávárdesh teñá!"

"Worms go in the milk,
From the milk into the garlic,
From the garlic into the water,
With the water to (your) father,
To the Nivasi,
He shall bind you with a rope,
Ninety-nine (yards long).[36]

The most intriguing part of this recipe perhaps is the description of the order in which the energies are to combine: the energies of the "worms" are to first go into the wolf's milk, a flowering herb also known as spurge that contains a poisonous, milky sap. Then the energies are directed into the garlic, then into the water, then into the Nivasi, a powerful water-spirit. Rather than combining the energies of the "worms" with the energy of the water and thus the Nivasi straightaway, it's recommended to instead send the essence of the "worms" first into the wolf's milk and then through the garlic before

36   Charles Godfrey Leland, *Gypsy Sorcery and Fortune Telling* (London: T. Fisher Unwin, 1891), 95, accessed January 2, 2012, http://www.sacred-texts.com/pag/gsft/gsft07.htm.

it reaches the water. Perhaps the action of the wolf's milk and the garlic is to weaken the "worms" and neutralize those energies a bit before the final action of the potion is effected and the "worms" are sent back to their origin and bound. If the energies of the malady were sent straight to the water without previously being altered or transformed in some fashion, perhaps the Nivasi would not be quite strong enough to bind these energies. By first combining the energy of the "worms" with the energies of the wolf's milk and the garlic, the infirmity is rendered more like the water into which it's next mixed, which in turn puts the "worms" at the mercy of the great water spirit Nivasi. We might here conclude that when trying to magickally bind or banish any extra strong or powerful energies, it might be helpful to mellow them out a bit first with some intermediary combining magick before you get to the heart of the spell.

Of course, getting rid of "worms" doesn't seem like the most exciting magickal goal to pursue, although I guess if you have them, it would be a totally different story! Assuming you're indeed worm-free for the moment, let's consider some of the deeper, more spiritual goals that can be achieved through the magick of mixing and combining energies. To give an example, sacred food and drink may have played an important and lofty role in the sacred Eleusinian Mysteries of the Greeks, acting to fuse and combine the spirits of the initiates to the energies and emotions of the great goddess Demeter. In Harold R. Willoughby's 1929 work *Pagan Regeneration*, a much earlier writing from Clement of Alexandria offering details of the Eleusinian mysteries is referenced:

> *Clement of Alexandria has preserved a formula that suggests the possibility of a different type of ritualistic observance. His statement is, "The password of the Eleusinian Mysteries is as follows: 'I have fasted, I have drunk the barley drink, I have taken things from the sacred chest, having tasted thereof; I have placed them into the basket and again from the basket into the chest." […] The fasting of the mystae corresponded to that of the sorrowing goddess Demeter who*

"sat smileless, nor tasted meat nor drink, wasting with long desire for her deep-bosomed daughter." Likewise the drinking of the barley drink corresponded to the breaking of her fast; for the goddess had refused a cup of sweet wine, "but she had them mix meal and water with the tender herb of mint, and give it to her to drink." This mixed potion the goddess accepted. Accordingly, in drinking a similar potation the mystae shared the cup from which the great goddess drank in her sorrow. It was a direct and sympathetic participation in the experiences of the goddess, an action expressive of attained fellowship with the deity.

Just what the eating of food from the chest meant to the participant is less obvious. Like the drinking of the barley drink, it was probably a sacrament of communion, and it may have implied an even more realistic communion than was involved in the act of drinking. If, as is most likely, the sacred food consisted of cereals, then the assimilation of this food meant a direct and realistic union with Demeter, the goddess of grain. It meant an incorporation of divine substance into the human body. However the idea was arrived at, this rite clearly involved a mystical communion by the act of eating, even as the barley drink stood for mystical fellowship through the act of drinking. Already emotionally united with Demeter through participation in her passion, the initiates now became realistically one with her by the assimilation of food and drink. [37]

The food and the barley, enchanted and combined with the essence of the goddess, become sacraments, and the ingestion of this holy sustenance acted to produce "a direct and realistic union with Demeter, the goddess of grain." We find in this testament that far from being confined to the spheres of love affairs, worms, and woe, magickally mixing energies through the

---

[37] Harold R. Willoughby, *Pagan Regeneration* (Chicago: The University of Chicago Press, 1929), Chapter 2, III, "The Greater Mysteries at Eleusis," accessed March 23, 2013, http://www.sacred-texts.com/cla/pr/pr04.htm.

use of food, drink, and other blended substances can be used to mesh one's energies with the very essence of the divine itself.

Common Threads and New Perspectives

Indeed, mixing magick is a useful technique and a versatile art. In this chapter, you've learned that energies can be mixed through dissolving, direct contact, and close proximity, and you've discovered how a written or spoken word can be used to convey intent into a magickal blend. You understand that potions and other forms of mixing magick can be used internally through ingestion or inhalation, or externally through direct application or close contact. From plants to animals to body-derived ingredients and inorganic objects, you've seen how certain ingredients for magickal mixtures might be chosen for their pharmaceutical properties, their symbolism, their sympathetic attributes, or their inherent magickal energies. You also understand that the order in which ingredients are combined can make a difference in a potion's efficacy, and that extra strong or baneful energies might be initially mellowed if desired before combining with the rest of your magickal mix.

Whether you're crafting an anointing oil to increase your wisdom and wit, or making a meal to unite your heart with that of the goddess, the mixtures of energies you create can be your own personal recipes, your own ways of expressing the intentions of your mind and soul. Make your combining spells reflect the dreams and goals that are uniquely *you*, and the magick you blend will manifest in just the right mix.

Potion Making and Mixing Magick Spells

Now you're ready to try some potion making and mixing magick of your own. Here are a couple of ideas for inspiration.

Super Magick Super Sandwich

To create a magickal sandwich to help you achieve your goals and intentions, select corresponding ingredients from the list below. You might make a sandwich to help you achieve health, wealth, happiness, or other desires. Decide specifically what each layer of the sandwich will represent, what energies it will contribute to the overall mix. Then select the sequence of the sandwich making accordingly. For instance, if your sandwich is designed to temper anger, you might find it fitting to add black pepper, a representative of anger or other forms of negativity, between ingredient layers symbolic of peace, or happiness. A suitable order in this hypothetical example might be first avocado to symbolize peace, then black pepper to represent negativity, then tomato to signify happiness. In this way, the anger is mellowed by being literally sandwiched between two peaceful, positive energies.

Here are some ingredients to consider including in your Super Magick Super Sandwich, along with some of their attributes and benefits. You don't have to use all these ingredients, of course—just select a few that seem most appropriate. You might also add spices, additional vegetables, or condiments chosen for color, flavor, shape, or magickal merit:

BREADS

Rye: Truth, strength

Wheat: Tenacity, strength, success, growth, stability

Pumpernickel: Spiritual communication, psychic awareness, swiftness, transformation

Flax: Luck, health, protection, strength

Whole Grain (any): Wholeness, completion, unity, energy, magickal power

VEGETABLES

Olives: Love, health, wealth, sensuality, passion

Tomato: Love, happiness, friendship, calming, cheer

Yellow Onion: Strength, health, defense

White Onion: Purification, strength, health, defense

Red Onion: Strength, defense, sweetness and love in the midst of adversity

Mushrooms: Spirit communication, dream magick, wisdom

Avocado: Peace, calming, sensuality

Watercress: Spirituality, emotion, love, dream magick

Kale: Purification, defense, strength, health

Sprouts: New growth, new beginnings, increased vitality, energy

Cucumbers: Calming, peace, purification

Pickles: Cheer, peace, purification, truth, banishing

EXTRAS

Cheese: Abundance, growth, binding, transformation, patience, fertility

Salt: Purification, defense, truth, happiness, energy, power

Black Pepper: Strength, defense, banishing, negativity, depression, sadness, anxiety, fear

Mustard: Banishing, defense, truth, strength

Mayonnaise: Fertility, binding, attracting

CLASSICS

Honey: Love, dream magick, sweetness, fertility, growth, health, friendship, inspiration, passion

Peanut Butter: Stability, strength, tenacity, the power of Earth, the underworld, hidden treasures

Strawberry Jam: Love, luck, happiness, friendship

Orange Marmalade: Solar energies, happiness, strength, confidence, power, vitality

Apple Butter: Love, luck, happiness, dream magick, friendship, health, calming

Grape Jelly: Abundance, prosperity, passion, fertility, joy

Select your ingredients, then jot down your general recipe. Place everything you'll need on your work surface. A muffin tin works great for sorting and storing sliced veggies, condiments, and other sandwich fixings. If you like, toast the bread you've selected—just don't forget to enchant your toaster first in homage to the late, great Polynesian sorcerer Kiki!

Clear your head, empower your ingredients with the respective attributes you desire, then begin assembling your sandwich. Think about your intention as you add each ingredient and combine it with the other energies in the recipe. Once assembled, your magickal sandwich is ready to use. Take a bite and activate the magick.

Personal Magnetism Power Potion

Try creating a custom blended potion for increasing your own personal magnetism and power. Depending on the ingredients you select, your Personal Magnetism Power Potion can be used either internally or externally. The recipe suggested below is intended for an external, non-edible potion, but it can be adapted into a drinkable blend by substituting safe, edible ingredients for the suggested non-food ingredients. If you do choose to make this potion for internal use, just be positive that you've adapted the recipe accordingly and that all your ingredients are absolutely 100% non-toxic and edible.

Begin by choosing a favorite cup or container in which to blend your potion. Select a container with a fairly wide mouth, as this will make it much easier to add the ingredients. A tight-closing lid is also a good feature, though it's not necessary if you prefer to make your magickal mixtures in single-use quantities.

Choose a word or symbol to represent the overall effect you're hoping to achieve with your power potion. It might be a word or symbol that expresses a quality you'd like to cultivate, a personal mantra, or a symbol of a goddess or other deity. Using honey and a toothpick, write or draw your word or symbol on the inside of your potion container.

Next, fill the container with pure, fresh water. Spring water works great. Place in the water a small magnet, then add to this a very personal ingredient to provide your own energetic signature. This might be a piece of your hair, a thread from your favorite dress, or a tiny drop of saliva. Next, add to the potion an ingredient chosen for its physical effects. Chamomile might be included to encourage a sense of calm, for instance, while mint or eucalyptus might be included for their invigorating properties. Finally, add an ingredient chosen for its symbolism, an emblem or substance that represents an energy you would like to invoke in yourself or a goal you would like to achieve. For instance, if you want greater leadership qualities, you might choose to add a jade stone, symbolic of authority and respect. If wealth is what you're after, you might add a shiny coin to your potion to represent money and prosperity. If you wish to be more loving, you might include a rose petal or a silver heart charm taken from a bracelet.

Once all the ingredients are added, swirl the potion clockwise, making a number of circles equal to your number of years on earth. Wrap the container in a piece of your clothing for safe keeping, taking care to seal the top or store it upright so it doesn't spill. Your potion is now ready for use. If you've crafted a nontoxic edible blend, simply ingest it straight or add it to food or drink. If your potion contains any non-food ingredients that aren't safe to eat, simply use the potion externally wherever and whenever it's needed. You might use your inedible potions to anoint your home, body, clothes, keys, or other personal effects. Anoint your pulse points with the magickal mixture, sprinkle a bit in your shoes, or place a few drops on your jewelry for an extra boost of personal magnetism and power anytime you need it.

Points to Ponder

- When mixing energies, do you think the order in which ingredients are added makes a difference? Why or why not?

- Might astrological timing be considered when performing mixing magick? Would a cheering potion created during a new moon work a little differently than a cheering potion blended during a full moon? What might the difference be, and could this effect be altered or manipulated with the addition of other ingredients?

- This chapter discussed the use of potions and other forms of mixing magick for the purposes of gaining bravery, wisdom, healing, and more. What other applications of magick to combine energies can you think of?

- Can infusing oneself with courage or other qualities through the ingestion of magickally charged food really be described as a combining of energies? Why or why not? What happens to the energy of the foods we ingest? Is some of the energy absorbed into the body? Is the energy of food and drink all physical, or might there also be a spiritual or magickal component?

- Besides mixing energies through the blending of foods and potions, what other mediums for combining magick can you think of? Might a collage made of various images glued together be classified as mixing magick? Could a bracelet made with multiple beads selected for their attributes be a medium for a spell to combine energies? How about a homemade patchwork quilt to foster friendly family relations and cooperation?

- This chapter mentioned several ways potions can be used externally, including administration through contact with the skin or through the bottom of a shoe. Can you think of other ways a witch might employ a potion externally?

- In some of the recipes presented in this chapter, energies were combined through the agents of dissolving, blending, mixing, and proximity. What other ways to combine one energy with another might there be? For what purposes might you use such magick?

three

The Art of Containing Energies: Magick to Have and to Hold

Now that you've mastered mixing magick, let's focus on magick intended to *confine* energies rather than combine them. Whether you wish to trap an unfriendly ghost or store some luck within a lucky charm, knowing how to do magick to contain energy is a skill quite useful to a witch. Through containing magick, energies can be held in one place, bound into restriction, or simply kept close by in order to attract desired vibrations or impart specific attributes. In this chapter, we'll take a look at some magickal techniques for containing energies that have been successfully employed throughout the world by magicians past, then we'll try putting these tricks to the test in the here and now.

Containing Magick Around the World

A containing spell might take a variety of outward forms, be it a talisman, an enchanted jar, or even a mock coffin. In ancient Egypt, images of the divine placed inside a miniature casket made for a magick spell to procure an afterlife. Wood carvings called Ptah-Seker-Ausar figures represented an important trinity of gods ruling over the life, death, and afterlife of the individual human being. These were set into rectangular wooden stands resembling coffins, and then placed in the tombs of the dead. Ptah, Seker, and Ausar (aka Osiris) were the gods of sunrise, the night sun, and resurrection, respectively, and it was believed that these deities together could work together to help the souls of the dead continue on after bodily demise. In E. A. Wallis Budge's 1901 work *Egyptian Magic*, a description of the use of Ptah-Seker-Ausar figures is given that nicely illuminates some of the finer points of symbolism. Budge writes:

> *Now the life of a man upon earth was identified with that of the sun; he "opened" or began his life as Ptah, and after death he was "shut in" or "coffined," like it also. But the sun rises again when the night is past, and, as it begins a new life with renewed strength and vigour, it became the type of the new life which the Egyptian hoped to live in the world beyond the grave. But the difficulty was how to obtain the protection of Ptah, Seker, and Osiris, and how to make them do for the man that which they did for themselves, and so secure their attributes. To attain this end a figure was fashioned in such a way as to include the chief characteristics of the forms of these gods, and was inserted in a rectangular wooden stand which was intended to represent the coffin or chest out of which the trinity Ptah-Seker-Ausar came forth. On the figure itself and on the sides of the stand were inscribed prayers on behalf of the man for whom it was made, and the Egyptian believed that these prayers caused the might and powers of the three gods to come and dwell in the wooden figure. But in order to make the stand of the figure as much like a coffin as possible, a small portion of the body of the deceased was carefully mummified and placed in it, and it was thought that if the three gods protected and preserved that*

piece, and if they revivified it in due season, the whole body would
be protected, and preserved, and revivified. [38]

This example reveals a belief that at least a measure of the very essence of the gods can be brought into an object through magickal means. Through inscribed prayers, the "might and powers" of the three gods is enticed to enter into the wooden figure, which in effect animates the object, infusing it with energy and life. A piece of flesh from the corpse formerly belonging to the soul to be assured resurrection was then inserted into the mock coffin along with the mock gods. This act of containing a portion of energy of the dead person within the energy of the coffin—which itself now contains the energies of the gods through the containing action of the prayer inscriptions, provides a sort of triple-layered containment system that holds firmly in place the energetic essences required for the spell.

Another example of containing magick is the Taoist practice of demon-trapping. In his 1893 work *Chinese Buddhism*, Joseph Edkins writes:

> *The power of expelling demons from haunted houses and localities,*
> *is believed to belong chiefly to the hereditary chief of the Tauists* [sic],
> *Chang Tien-shï, and subordinately to any Tauist priest. To expel*
> *demons he wields the sword that is said to have come down, a priceless*
> *heirloom, from his ancestors of the Han dynasty. All demons fear this*
> *sword. He who wields it, the great Tauist magician, can catch demons*
> *and shut them up in jars. These jars are sealed with a "charm" (fu). I*
> *have heard that at the home of this chief of wizards on the Dragon and*
> *Tiger mountain in the province of Kiang-si, there are many rows of*
> *such jars, all of them supposed to hold demons in captivity.* [39]

---

38   E. A. Wallis Budge, *Egyptian Magic* (London: Kegan, Paul, Trench and Trübner & Co., 1901), 84–85, accessed March 1, 2012, http://www.sacred -texts.com/egy/ema/ema05.htm.

39   Rev. Joseph Edkins, DD, *Chinese Buddhism: a Volume of Sketches, Historical, Descriptive, and Critical* (London: Kegan Paul, Trench, Trübner and Company, 1893), 387, accessed January 5, 2012, http://openlibrary.org/ books/OL23286290M/Chinese_Buddhism.

The wizard, the charm, the sword—the power of all these work in unison to create one fearsome combination powerful enough to ensnare a demon. The wizard and the sword take care of the initial intimidation and show of power needed to scare the demon into the trap. Once in, the jar is sealed with a charm and the demon is therein contained. In the mention of the rows of demon traps kept at the chief wizard's home on the Dragon and Tiger mountain, we might infer that jars are a solid, practical choice for containing magick, capable of sealing away energies for presumably as long as is desired. Who would have guessed that a good old-fashioned jar is just as useful in preserving demons as it is in preserving jellies and jams?

A somewhat similar method of spirit-trapping through containment was practiced by the Ibibio, a large tribe centered in southeastern Nigeria. In her 1915 work *Woman's Mysteries of a Primitive People*, D. Amaury Talbot writes of a ritual in which an *Idiong*, a type of diviner-priest, traps the ghost of an interfering ex-husband; the "chop" here mentioned is simply Nigerian slang for "food":

> When the thoughts of a widow have already turned to another
> wooer she is terrified lest the spirit of her former husband should
> return and seek to draw her after him to the ghost realm. Should
> she have reason to suppose that such is the case, she goes to an
> Idiong man who has a great reputation for second sight. By his
> advice, "chop" is cooked and placed in one corner of her room.
> The priest takes up a position immediately before this, and stands
> calling upon the name of the ghost. Close to the place where the
> food is laid some member of the family crouches, holding a strong
> pot, preferably of iron, tilted forward ready to invert over the
> one in which the food is served. When the Idiong man makes a
> sign that the ghost is busy eating, and that, in enjoyment of the
> feast, the latter has temporarily forgotten to look after his safety,

the second pot is clapped over the first, and both are then bound firmly together, thus keeping the spirit imprisoned between.[40]

Instead of a powerful sword and a powerful incantation being needed, we here find that a pot of yummy, tempting food is sufficient distraction to occupy the spirit so that it's ripe for the catching. The Ibibio *Idiong* simply claps a pot over the top of the spirit while it's busy enjoying the chop, and voila, the wayward ghost of the jealous ex-husband is now contained. We can see in this method the value of not only simplicity and practicality, but also the value of the distraction. The spirit must be put off its guard before it can be captured, and here we find that the food as well as the calling of the spirit's name and the use of the two pots provide the practical and magickal backbone on which the method seems to rely.

A very simple and straightforward method of containing a ghost was employed in Jamaica, also. In a 1932 work, Joseph J. Williams gives a description of how the people accomplished the catching of a person's "shadow" upon their death, a practice deemed necessary to prevent the spirit of the dead from pestering the living. Though clearly written from the perspective of an outsider, the text nonetheless provides us with an intriguing glimpse into a very hands-on way to contain a ghost:

I have more than once watched the process from a very short distance, near enough, in fact, to be able to hear all that was said, and to watch carefully most that was done, as the actors, for such I must call them, scrambled and grasped at empty nothingness…

After a time, one more "forward" than the rest would claim to have caught the prey, only to be greeted with cries of scorn: "'Im get away! See 'im dah!" Whereupon the scuffle would start anew.

---

40   D. Amaury Talbot, *Woman's Mysteries of a Primitive People* (London: Cassell and Company, LTD., 1915), 174–175, accessed November 12, 2012, http://www.sacred-texts.com/afr/wmp/wmp13.htm.

*Eventually when all of them were breathless… the feat would
be accomplished by some belligerent individual, who would clasp his
hands and let out a veritable Scream of defiance: "Me got 'im! Me
got 'im!" with such vehemence that he would literally shout down
all protests to the contrary… Then a box or at times a small coffin
would be produced and with much ado, not perhaps without a final
effort to escape, the poor "shadow" would be securely fastened in and
properly "laid" to be buried later at the funeral.* [41]

Although the battle is hard-won, the mere physical strength, agility, determination, and speed of the spirit-catchers is enough to prevail over the escaping "shadow." The box or small coffin here used is parallel to the jars used in the Taoist demon traps and to the pots used in the Ibibio ghost-trapping procedure. Again, we see the use of a material object to contain a ghost or "shadow." The "shadow" is in this case forced into its appointed container not by a chief or a priest, but by a regular everyday somebody, a somebody who's probably without even the smallest piece of chop or tiniest magickal sword to help distract the rogue spirit and slow its getaway. We might infer here that though special skill can come in handy, sheer willpower and a team spirit is enough in a pinch to catch and contain a wayward ghost.

To the mystically minded people of the South Pacific islands, magickally containing a spirit was a bit more involved. In an 1855 work by Sir George Grey, the author includes the following procedure:

*The priests next dug a long pit, termed the pit of wrath, into which
by their enchantments they might bring the spirits of their enemies,
and hang them and destroy them there; and when they had dug the
pit, muttering the necessary incantations, they took large shells in*

---

41   Joseph J. Williams, *Voodoos and Obeahs: Phases of West India Witchcraft*
(New York: Lincoln Mac Veagh, Dial Press Inc., 1932), 152–153, accessed
March 23, 2013, http://www.sacred-texts.com/afr/vao/vao07.htm.

their hands to scrape the spirits of their enemies into the pit with,
whilst they muttered enchantments; and when they had done this,
they scraped the earth into the pit again to cover them up, and
beat down the earth with their hands, and crossed the pit with
enchanted cloths, and wove baskets of flax-leaves, to hold the spirits
of the foes which they had thus destroyed, and each of these acts they
accompanied with proper spells. [42]

The method employed in this instance of containing magick is quite laborious. Not only does a giant pit need digging, but also enchantments must be uttered to tempt and trick the spirits of the enemies to come near. Further, the spirits must then be scraped into the hole, symbolically "hung," and finally buried, all parts of the procedure accompanied by additional spells and utterances. The spirits of the enemies are at last, through this multiple step process, contained within the dreaded "pit of wrath." The containing magick here performed is accomplished through a number of elements: the will of the magicians, the strength of the incantations, and the force of the dirt, cloth, and flax leaf baskets are used in conjunction to trap the spirits inside the mock grave.

We can identify here also the application of imitative magick; in the mock burying of invisible enemies within the mock grave, the spirits of the foes are symbolically contained, and through this imitative action a belief is expressed that reality will soon shift to match.

Containing magick was employed to combat enemies in Ireland, as well. In *Irish Druids and Old Irish Religions*, author James Bonwick quotes an earlier Irish text that makes reference to the restraint of an enemy by way of a sea storm:

42   Sir George Grey, *Polynesian Mythology and Ancient Traditional History of the New Zealanders: As Furnished by Their Priests and Chiefs* (London: John Murray, 1855), 125–126, accessed March 23, 2013, http://www.sacred-texts.com/pac/grey/grey13.htm.

In the Story of Deirdri it is written, "As Conor saw this, he went
to Cathbad the Druid, and said to him, 'Go, Cathbad, unto the
sons of Usnach, and play Druidism upon them.' This was done.
He had recourse to his intelligence and art to restrain the children
of Usnach, so that he laid them under enchantment, that is, by
putting around them a viscid sea of whelming waves." [43]

We find in this text a different sort of way to work a containment charm, using the weather and the environment to one's benefit. By surrounding the enemies with a violent sea storm, they're effectively trapped and rendered harmless. We might gather from this example that strong, turbulent, or otherwise unwieldy forces can be used to create a magickal perimeter in which to confine and contain energies marked for isolation. We might further infer that the act of magickally encircling something is in itself a way to contain energy. Besides a raging sea, what other energies can you think of that might be effective in creating a perimeter of power within which to contain a foe?

A similar yet different magickal method of containing through encircling was performed by the Pennsylvania Dutch. In order to keep cattle contained within a person's property and charm it into returning if ever it should wander, the following technique was employed:

Take a handful of salt, go upon your fields and make your cattle walk
three times around the same stump or stone, each time keeping the
same direction; that is to say, you must three times arrive at the same
end of the stump or stone at which you started from, and then let
your cattle lick the salt from the stump or stone. [44]

---

43   James Bonwick, *Irish Druids and Old Irish Religions* (London: Griffeth, Farran, 1894), 51, accessed June 5, 2012, http://www.sacred-texts.com /pag/idr/idr12.htm.

44   John George Hohman, *Long Lost Friend* (1820; trans., Camden, NJ: Star and Book Novelty Company, 1828), "Another Method of Making Cattle Return Home," accessed March 23, 2013, http://www.sacred-texts.com/ ame/pow/pow047.htm.

Although the circle of containment is in this case created by the mundane motion of the circling cow rather than by the magickal manifestation of a ring of raging seas, the basic action is the same: energies are restricted and confined through the simple expedient of casting a circle of power around them.

The Pennsylvania Dutch also used containing magick for healing. One remedy runs as follows:

Let the sick person, without having conversed with anyone, put water in a bottle before sunrise, close it up tight, and put it immediately in some box or chest. lock it and stop up the keyhole; the key must be carried in one of the pockets for three days, as nobody dare have it except the person who puts the bottle with water in the chest or box.[45]

The charm described here produces its healing effect by containing and isolating the energies of the illness, an act of imitative magick that symbolically separates the sickness from the person. When the sick person fills the bottle with water, through the combining principle of close proximity, that water is infused with the very essence of their infirmity. By sealing the bottle tight and locking it up in a dark box or chest for several days, the sickness is symbolically contained and isolated to the point of extinguish, just as a flame deprived of oxygen cannot last. We can see in this example that it's the symbolism and imitative actions incorporated into the magick that enables many a containing spell to work.

One well-known, oft-employed, and very straightforward type of containing magick is the use of talismans or amulets, objects which act as literal containers for holding and storing magickal power. Designed to contain a charm, spell or spirit, talismans and amulets are intended to either attract desired energies or repel undesired energies. Though technically

45   John George Hohman, "Another Remedy to be Applied when Anyone is Sick," accessed March 23, 2013, http://www.sacred-texts.com/ame/pow/pow007.htm.

and traditionally a talisman does the former while an amulet does the latter, the terms are today used pretty much interchangeably.

Popular throughout the world, talismans and amulets vary greatly in both form and function. The Yoruba tribe of West Africa, for example, employed amulets called *onde* for protection of people, property, and other endeavors. While the specific placement of these amulets was of the utmost importance, they could be crafted out of virtually anything. Even a stick could be used, though bones, teeth, claws, horns, and shells were favored.[46] Body-derived ingredients, so useful in so many forms of magick, are particularly useful mediums for containing magick, too. The amulets were placed according to their function: an onde for personal protection would be worn on the body, while an onde for the protection of property might be attached directly to the home.[47] Proximity of the contained energy, we can gather, allows for those energies to affect the essence of whatever is near.

Onde were originally thought to function through housing an indwelling spirit, but over time the idea evolved, and eventually the onde came to be considered as simply the vehicle through which a spirit can act. In comparing these two different perspectives on the onde, we see a difference in the design of the amulets while the function remains the same. Whether the onde permanently houses an indwelling spirit or merely acts as a channel through which the spirit can momentarily exercise its sway, in either scenario, a portion of the energy of the spirit is contained at least temporarily within the onde, it's power focused and localized within the amulet.

The only difference is that in the latter case, the spirit is just passing through the onde, rather than taking up long-term residence. This difference highlights the fact that containing magick need not be absolutely complete: even a sieve fraught with holes can still keep in the chunks.

---

46   Rev. Robert Hamill Nassau, *Fetichism in West Africa* (1904; repr., Charleston, SC: BiblioBazaar, LLC, 2008), 75–76.

47   A. B. Ellis, *Yoruba-Speaking Peoples of the Slave Coast of West Africa* (1894; repr., Charleston, SC: Forgotten Books, 2007), 97–98.

The spirits aren't necessarily *trapped* in the onde, but they're contained enough to be held by the magician and used to advantage.

The Druids also made use of talismans to contain magickal power. One interesting example was called a serpent's egg, an oval-shaped crystal that was thought to bring victory and protection to the person who bore it.[48] Often worn around the neck as a mark of dignity and distinction, the serpent's egg talisman worked its magick by imparting its own mystical attributes to the wearer. Up until the late 1700s, the charms were popular in parts of England, Wales, and Scotland.[49]

The magick of the serpent's egg talismans didn't rely on the power of an indwelling god or visiting spirit as was the case with the Yoruba *onde*. Instead, the magickal attributes and desired properties of the talismans were inherent, naturally present in the unique shape and composition of the crystal "eggs." The Druidic use of the serpent's egg talisman does parallel the Yoruban use of the onde in one way, however. In wearing the serpent's egg—a personal talisman—suspended from a cord around the neck, the Druids share the same logic as employed by the Yoruba in placing their onde. By keeping the energies contained within the serpent's egg in close proximity to the body, those energies are held in close enough range to have a magickal effect and impart their virtues exactly where needed, just as the Yoruba might attach to the side of a house an onde for the protection of property.

The Inuit also used talismans and amulets for containing energy, and like the Druids, they took particular care in the choice of materials used to craft these magickal objects, preferring substances thought to have inherent power. In an 1875 work by Henry Rink, Inuit amulets are described:

48   Peter Berresford Ellis, *A Brief History of the Druids* (New York: Carroll and Graf Publishers, 2002), 59–60.

49   James Bonwick, *Irish Druids and Old Irish Religions* (London: Griffith, Farran, 1894), 47–48, accessed June 5, 2012, http://www.sacred-texts.com/pag/idr/idr10.htm.

The efficacy of an amulet depends firstly on the nature of the original thing or matter from whence it has been derived. To serve this purpose, certain animals or things which had belonged to or been in contact with certain persons or supernatural beings were chiefly chosen; and sometimes, but more rarely, also objects which merely by their appearance recalled the effect expected from the amulet, such as figures of various objects . . . Although the articles thus used had a power of their own because of their origin, they still required the application of a serrat, which was pronounced by him who gave the amulet to its final proprietor. If it was only to be used in particular cases, a special serrat was also required in order to make it work; and in some cases, when the owner happened not to have the amulet at hand, he might have recourse to invocation. [50]

We see here that in addition to choosing an inherently powerful object with which to craft the amulet, the principle of sympathetic magick as well as the contagion principle can also be basis for selection. We find also that the Inuit amulet may require activation: a *serrat*, a type of spoken spell or charm that might be recited or sung, is needed in order to make the amulets "work." It's mentioned that such a serrat can be used to activate the amulet even when it's not close by. The amulet's link to the serrat gives the Inuit magician an advantage. For one, if the amulet is stolen or otherwise found in the hands of another person, it will remain inactive unless the new owner just happens to know the associated serrat necessary to unlock the amulet's magickal power. Another advantage is that the amulet does not rely on close proximity to have an effect. The magickal energy held within the amulet can be summoned forth and called into action by the reciting of the serrat anytime, anywhere. The serrat provides a key to the containing magick, an "on" button that powers up and cues the energy within the amulet when it's time to act.

---

50   Henry Rink, *Tales and Traditions of the Eskimo* (Edinburgh, London: William, Blackwood, and Sons, 1875), 52–53, accessed April 4, 2012, http://www.sacred-texts.com/nam/inu/tte/tte1–4.htm.

Common Threads and New Perspectives

From a spell packed into a talisman to a ring of raging seas around a foe, containing magick is both versatile and effective in its forms and in its functions. In this chapter, we've seen how containing magick can be used to hold in place both spirits and desired energies. We've examined how inscriptions, incantations, spiritual strength, sheer willpower, and even distraction can be used to entice an energy or entity into its appointed container, be it a mock grave, an amulet, or a demon trap. We've seen also that containing magick is often multi-layered, designed with several elements all working in conjunction, and we've learned that imitative and symbolic actions, words, and intentions are often at the heart of this type of magick. We've seen that while some containing spells don't depend on an actual, physical container in which to house the energy to be held (for example, a circular motion can be utilized instead), others do require a material component. We've discovered that the object chosen to act as this literal container might be selected for its inherent attributes, its sympathetic symbolism, or its power derived through the contagion principle—for instance, a rock found in a sacred stream might be deemed powerful by the fact of its proximity to the holy waters. We've noted also, however, that an object used for containing magick doesn't necessarily have to be special: a stick, a couple of cooking pots, nearly anything really, can be used as a physical container for spiritual energies.

Through the many and varied methods of containing magick, a witch can indeed achieve a multitude of aims, from quarantining a threat to securing good luck to catching a ghost. Try using containing magick in creative ways. For instance, you might create a talisman designed to store away for future use the leftover energy that lingers after a major spellcasting, or you might attempt to cast a containment charm on the spread of gun violence, or pollution. The only limit to the magickal energies you can contain is your own imagination, willpower, skill, and daring.

Containing Magick Spells

Ready to do your own containing magick? Here are a couple of spells to try. As you work through these methods, see how they compare to the traditional techniques you read about in this chapter.

Ghost-Catching Spell

If you've got a wayward ghost in your house, choosing whether or not to get rid of it can be a tough decision. If it's a friendly ghost, you might not mind the company; if it's an annoying or frightening spirit, however, you'd probably rather they move someplace else. The first thing to do if you suspect your house is haunted is to attempt to communicate with the suspected stowaway spirit or spirits. You can use a spirit board, tarot cards, or automatic writing to accomplish this. If you decide after communicating with the haunting spirit that you would like it to relocate, the following methods of ghost containment may prove helpful.

If it's a generally friendly, seemingly cooperative spirit you're dealing with, a crystal, dish of salt, or even a glass of water can be an effective vehicle for friendly ghost relocation. Let the spirit know your intentions to move it to a different location, and invite it to enter into the chosen medium. You might use additional prayers and chants to help entice the spirit into the container. When you sense the spirit has entered the substance, envision a circle of energy surrounding it, keeping it contained and bound within the ghost trap. Take it to a place that feels appropriate and release it: simply shake the crystal, or scatter or pour the water or salt. Let the spirit know that it is free to go, released from the substance to cross over into the other side more fully, or to remain wandering the earth at a location other than your home. If you're dealing with an unfriendly spirit, the method will be a bit different. One effective technique is to use a mirror. Place a mirror flat on the floor in the room where you sense the most ghostly activity. Run your finger in a counterclockwise spiral around the mirror, starting on the outer edge and working in toward the center. At the center, make a single dot with your fingertip—this is the portal your ghost will enter. If you like, use a spirit-attracting herb or oil to trace the spiral and dot. Envision the spirit being inescapably drawn into the mirror. Invite it to enter with complimentary words acknowledging the ghost's greatness—in other words, sweet talk it! Place spicy or extra pungent food around the perimeter of the mirror to further tempt the spirit. Leave the mirror in place for a week or so and see if the ghost activity is now limited to the room in which the mirror is located. Once this occurs, wrap the mirror in a blanket and take it somewhere far away from your home. Dig a hole, smash the mirror, quickly toss the pieces into the hole, and cover it with dirt. Shake out the blanket thoroughly and wash and dry it immediately.

Circle of Containment Talisman Creation Spell

This spell can be used to create a talisman to contain and store magickal power to be released on command when needed, be it during a challenging ritual or a nerve-wracking exam. The first thing you'll need to do is select an object to use as the talisman. You might choose an object for its inherent power, such as a crystal, or you might select a symbolic token such as a star-shaped charm. You might choose an object found in a sacred place, like a small jar of dirt taken from a pretty mountaintop, for instance. If you can't find anything special, you might decide to use any old random item—whatever's handy or convenient—like that pencil on your desk, for instance.

Once you've selected the object to become your talisman, place it in the center of your magickal workspace. Begin by casting a circle as usual, invoking the elements as well as any deities or spirits whose attributes or abilities you wish to be imparted to the talisman. When you sense that all the summoned energies are indeed present, begin walking in inward spirals toward the center of the circle where the talisman lies. Draw in the energy present in the circle as you do so, shrinking the circle's perimeter with each revolution. Envision the power of the elements, deities, and spirits spiraling closer and closer toward the talisman, chanting as you do so, "I draw in the circle; I draw in the power!" Eventually, your circle will be super-tiny, encasing only the talisman. At this point, use your will and a tap of your wand or fingertips to direct the power contained in the mini-circle to enter completely into the talisman. Imagine a new circle of pure, white light enveloping the talisman, sealing in the charm but allowing the power now within it to glow and grow, strong and bright. As you do so, chant, "I draw out the circle, I draw out the power!" Your talisman is now activated. It can be carried on your person or kept on your altar as a general magickal strengthener. While it will provide a measure of magickal power from now on, an extra blast of energy can be obtained from the talisman anytime by uttering the charm used as the final chant: "I draw out the circle, I draw out the power!"

Points to Ponder

- This chapter discussed how to contain energies using various methods such as encircling the energy to be contained with another, more powerful energy, or encasing the energy within a solid physical object. Can you think of any additional techniques for magickally containing energies that weren't discussed in this chapter?

- If you were aiming to contain an angry energy by confining it within a perimeter of another, more powerful energy, what are some particular qualities you feel would be beneficial to incorporate into this ring of power?

- While some of the talismans discussed in this chapter were quite specific in the choice of materials used to house the power of the charm, we found that other talismans can be crafted with little or no importance given to the substance or object used in its creation. Do you think care should be taken in choosing the item or ingredient to act as a talisman? Might some substances be better at containing very strong and harmful energies, for instance, while other substances might prove superior at housing more mellow essences? Could *any* object be used in a pinch as a talismanic container for energy? Why or why not?

- Could a containing spell possibly be used to entice a lost dog to return home? How might a person cast such magick?

- With containing magick, you have a versatile tool to use in a variety of situations, from restricting a dangerous enemy to keeping your budget within its means. What other circumstances can you imagine in which an act of containing magick might be of benefit?

Four

Ties that Bind

As illustrated in our last chapter on containing magick, the ability to ensnare or otherwise control energy is a magickal skill that can prove quite useful in a variety of situations. Tried and true and popular for ages, the art of tying a simple knot is one way spellcasters can achieve these aims. Operating primarily on principles of binding or containment, the practice of making magick by tying knots is widespread. Throughout the world, knots have been used for magickal purposes ranging from calming the seas to stopping an enemy, from catching a thief to stealing a heart. In this chapter, we'll explore some examples of knot magick from around the world, and we'll learn some new techniques for making our own modern knot magick more effective.

Knot Magick Around the World

As far as magickal techniques go, knot magick is fairly easy to master. Through the straightforward acts of tying and untying, magick can be not only rendered, but also released. In *The Welsh Fairy Book*, a 1908 work by W. Jenkyn Thomas, the simple use of a knot to hold an "ace up the sleeve" for later use is described. Although the scene recounted is fictional as well as somewhat comical, it nonetheless does well to illustrate the basic effect and benefit of a knot charm:

> *It was impossible to overcome the smugglers in a fray, for each*
> *of them carried about with him a black fly tied in a knot of his*
> *neckerchief. When their strength failed them in the fight they*
> *undid the knots of their cravats, and the flies flew at the eyes of*
> *their opponents and blinded them.* [51]

Whether these are real, living, actual flies or metaphorical flies symbolic of powerful energy isn't specified, but whether they're flies or the Force, the message is the same: power can be reserved in a knot and released by the untying of that knot. Though the book from which this story comes is a compilation of fairy tales, the real practice of knot magick is far from fiction.

From the Welsh to the Roma to the Zoroastrians, knots have been used by many people around the world to contain, bind, and store energy. Energy is held within the twisted form of the knot, and this power can be set free by a simple untying action if ever the desire or need to do so arises.

In Europe, witches were accused of using knots to bind everything from cattle to thunderstorms. While there was a definite tendency to blame things on the witch, as it were, witches were just as often petitioned rather than prosecuted for their magickal charms. Knot charms were seen as both objects to fear and precious commodities, and many non-witches came to rely on them. In *Folk-Lore of the Isle of Man*, an 1891 work by A. W. Moore, the author makes reference to a much earlier text describing a knot charm that became quite popular among sailors around the islands near Scotland, back in the days when the wind was the only fuel available to carry a person across the sea. Moore writes:

---

51   W. Jenkyn Thomas, *The Welsh Fairy Book* (1908; repr., Charleston, SC: BiblioBazaar, LLC, 2008), 167.

*It would seem that the inhabitants of Man and the other Western
Isles of Scotland had acquired a reputation for magical powers
at an early period ... we are told by Ranulph Higden that "In the
Ilonde of Mann is sortilege and witchcraft used; for women there
sell to shipmen wynde as it were closed under three knottes of
threde, so that the more wynde he would have the more knottes
he must undo."* [52]

While the sailors lived ultimately at the mercy to the sea, they could also purchase charms that allowed them to carry the winds around in a piece of knotted thread, to let loose as needed and at the strength desired. We see here illustrated how a knot charm can be more flexible than many other forms of binding and containing magick. The wind is not trapped indefinitely, but is only temporarily held until the sailor wishes it to be unleashed. It's worth noting that even though these knot charms were crafted by the landlubber women of the Isle of Man, they were considered perfectly effective for the sailors who bought them. We might infer from this fact a belief that knot charms can be operated and set into motion by anyone who happens to untie the charm and unloose the magick—which is a good reason to take care in choosing where to keep such a magickal object.

The idea of the three knots in this charm each containing its respective amount of wind is also intriguing, illuminating possibilities for the specific form and design of the magick. Separate winds might be contained in separate knots, or multiple winds might be contained within a single knot. As yet another possibility, the power of a single wind might be split up and divvied out among several knots, each knot binding a share of the wind's essence and energy.

Knot magick allows for binding in increments—a little energy here in this knot, a bit of power there in that knot. In this way, the magickal power

---

52   A. W. Moore, *Folk-Lore of the Isle of Man* (London: D. Nutt, 1891), 76, accessed
     June 1, 2012, http://www.sacred-texts.com/neu//celt/fim/fim08.htm.

contained via a knot charm can be unleashed at the force and timing of the magician's own choosing. In *The Golden Bough*, Sir James George Frazer describes the operation of a knot charm for wind crafted by Finnish wizards that does well to illustrate this principle:

> *The wind was enclosed in three knots; if they undid the first knot,*
> *a moderate wind sprang up; if the second, it blew a half gale; if*
> *the third, a hurricane.* [53]

The use of multiple knots in a single charmed object is not an idea exclusive to the sailing set. The Zoroastrians also used multiple knots in their mystical practice, though for very different purposes. An 1885 translation of the medieval Zoroastrian *Pahlavi Texts* gives the following description of the knots of the sacred girdle, a cord tied around the waist that was worn to help a worshiper of Ahura Mazda, the Zoroastrian supreme deity of light and wisdom, follow prescribed spiritual principles:

> *And those four knots with which they tie it on, are on this*
> *account, that it may give four attestations. The first knot is that*
> *which preserves constancy (qarâr), and gives attestation as to the*
> *existence, unity, purity, and matchlessness of the sacred being,*
> *the good and propitious. The second knot is that which gives*
> *attestation that it is the good religion of the Mazda-worshippers*
> *which is the word of the sacred being. The third knot is that which*
> *gives attestation as to the apostleship and mission (rasûlî) in the*
> *just ('haqq) Zaratust, the Spitamân. The fourth knot is that which*
> *adduces more pleasantly, gives assurance (iqrâr), and openly*
> *accepts that I should think of good, speak of good, and do good.*

---

53   Sir James George Frazer, *The Golden Bough* (1922; repr., New York: Bartleby.com, 2000), Chapter 5, Section 4, "The Magical Control of the Wind," accessed January 9, 2012, http://www.bartleby.com/196/13.html.

And from the whole I become established; and the pure, good religion is this, that I persist in those views. [54]

We see in the Zoroastrian sacred girdle the use of a knot for restraint: the first knot described "preserves constancy," ensuring faithfulness to the deity and to the religion. We see also the use of knots for safekeeping ideas and intentions. The second, third, and fourth knots are all described as "giving attestation," serving as symbols of one's dedication to certain important spiritual principles and goals. By housing the essence of these ideals within the girdle's knots and then encircling the waist of the Zoroastrian with this magickal energy, a charm is created that helps the adherent remain within the bounds of the Zoroastrian spiritual recommendations—"And from the whole I become established," the text states. We find here that not only can the magickal art of tying knots be used to bind outside energies like enemies and forces of nature, but it can also be used to bind the self, restricting behavior into desired or recommended boundaries.

The Roma also made use of knot magick, incorporating both naturally occurring knots as well as man-made knots into a variety of spells and charms. In *Gypsy Sorcery and Fortune Telling*, Charles Godfrey Leland includes a Roma charm that makes use of both a natural knot and an artificial knot to catch a thief:

If a man who is seeking for stolen goods finds willow twigs grown into a knot, he ties it up and says:
"Me avri pçándáv čoreskro báçht!"
"I tie up the thief's luck!" [55]

54   E. W. West, trans., *Pahlavi Texts, Part III, Sacred Books of the East, Volume 24* (New York: Clarendon, Oxford University Press, 1885), 270, accessed May 9, 2012, http://www.sacred-texts.com/zor/sbe24/sbe24098.htm.

55   Charles Godfrey Leland, *Gypsy Sorcery and Fortune Telling* (London: T. Fisher Unwin, 1891), 110, accessed January 2, 2012, http://www.sacred-texts.com/pag/gsft/gsft09.htm.

The naturally occurring willow knot, believed by the Roma to be fairy-made and thus naturally lucky, acts in this charm as a symbol of the unknown thief's good fortune. Through the act of tying up that knot within another knot, the energies therein symbolized are restricted, and the thief's luck becomes bound and contained within the artificial man-made knot. The Roma also held a belief that a person's luck could be undone by untying a willow knot while focusing on the foe in question;[56] here we find that instead of being untied, the willow knot turned symbol of the thief is made to affect bad luck by being further bound and contained within an additional knot. As usual in the arts of magick, there's more than one way to stir a cauldron.

Willow knots weren't only used to bind up the luck of thieves and foes; sometimes, they were used in the optimistic hope of bringing lovers closer together. Leland describes how the Roma make use of the naturally occurring willow knot to sway the affections:

> These willow-knots are much used in love-charms.
> To win the love of a maid, a man cuts one of them,
> puts it into his mouth, and says:—
> "T're báçt me çáv,
> T're baçt me piyáv,
> Dáv tute m're baçt,
> Káná tu mánge sál.
> I eat thy luck,
> I drink thy luck
> Give me that luck of thine,
> Then thou shalt be mine."
> Then the lover, if he can, secretly hides
> this knot in the bed of the wished-for bride.[57]

---

56   Charles Godfrey Leland, 110–111, accessed January 2, 2012, http://www
       .sacred-texts.com/pag/gsft/gsft09.htm.

57   *Ibid.*

By placing the willow knot in his or her mouth, the Roma forges a connection to be utilized once the knot is placed in the bed of the lover and begins to absorb and "pick up" the essence of the desired dreamer, thereby placing the dreamer within the will of the magician. We might infer from this example that knots used in knot magick can be pre-charmed beforehand, before being charged or filled with the energies which that knot is to bind.

The Roma weren't the only people to use knots for love magick. In a 1906 collection of European folklore, a knot charm to dream of one's future lover is described:

> *Thus girls when in a strange bed would, in years past, tie their*
> *garters nine times round the bedpost, and knit as many knots in*
> *them, repeating these lines by way of incantation—*
> *"This knot I knit, this knot I tie,*
> *To see my lover as he goes by,*
> *In his apparel and array,*
> *As he walks in every day;"*
> *there being various versions of this rhyme,*
> *one of which runs thus:—*
> *This knot I knit*
> *To know the thing I know not yet:*
> *That I may see*
> *The man that shall my husband be;*
> *How he goes and what he wears,*
> *And what he does all days and years."* [58]

Here, we again find intentions stored in the twists and turns of a knot, this time in the form of a knotted garter. Both the intention and the

---

58   T. F. Thiselton-Dyer, *Folk-Lore of Women* (Chicago: A. C. McClurg and Co., London: Elliot Stock, 1906), Chapter XXIII, accessed May 1, 2012, http://www.sacred-texts.com/wmn/fow/fow25.htm.

method for achieving it is clearly stated: "This knot I knit To know the thing I know not yet." By weaving one's intentions to dream of a future lover into the knots, the charm is set. It's then placed right where it's needed, close to the dreamer who will need to keep the intentions of the magick firmly held nearby whilst she or he sleeps. Here, the knot provides a sturdy container for a charm that needs to hold up in the mysterious and unpredictable realms of the dreamworld.

Another point to note is the choice of material in which to place the knots. A garter is a very personal item, often associated with sexuality and femininity. Variations of the charm are found in several nineteenth century collections of European folklore, and some versions call for a stocking to be knotted rather than a garter. In either case, the basic symbolism is the same. By using a personal item representative of intimacy, the intention of the knot charm is further expressed. We can learn from this custom that in knot magick, the wise witch will choose which strings to tie wisely. Perhaps certain colors of string or certain fabrics are ideal for particular forms of knot magick; perhaps using a personal item such as a piece of clothing or hair when doing a knot charm to bind an enemy would increase the charm's potency. By choosing the materials to be tied in knot magick with symbolism and energetic attributes in mind, another layer of magickal power is added to an already powerful spell.

Common Threads and New Perspectives

In this chapter, we've surveyed some ways in which magicians around the world have used knots to control, ensnare, reserve, restrain, harness, and restrict energy. We've seen that these actions can be applied against any number of forces, from the wind to a lover, from an intention to an enemy. We know that the magick encased in such a knot can be easily unleashed or undone through the simple expedient of untying, and we understand one advantage of the knot charm is in this flexibility. While materials used in knot magick may range from a naturally occurring willow knot to a simple piece of string, we're aware of the potential benefits in choosing a material that relates in some way to its intended purpose. We've learned that multiple energies can be bound into single knots or multiple knots, and that singular energies can be bound in increments, with power and essence distributed equally among several knots. Though ultimately simple and straightforward, like all magickal arts, so too can knot magick become as complicated and complex as you wish. All magick is a way of forging connections, and the ties that bind a knot charm can indeed run deep.

Knot Magick Spell

Now it's time to try your own powerful knot magick. Begin by deciding on a purpose for your knot charm. Do you have a bad habit you'd like to get under control, or is there an evil empire somewhere in the world that needs shutting down?

Once you've decided on the energies that need restricting, choose a string or other material in which to set your charm. Is the knot charm going to be used to attract a lover? If so, consider red or pink string, or a "romantic" material such as silk or satin for your spell. Is the knot charm intended to restrict an enemy, or another dangerous or baneful force? Consider tying your knots in "heavy" materials such as faux leather, vines, or even metal wire to bind up these powerful energies. Is your knot charm meant to store personal intentions, holding these energies close to your side? If so, you might choose strings or other materials with color symbolism in mind— just match the string color to your particular personal goal.

Once you've selected the material and the general intention of your spell, hold the string or whatever else you're using firmly in your hand. Think of the essence, the energies of the force you wish to bind, contain, or restrict. Consciously direct this energy into the thread. You'll want to actually *name* the string for the thing you're binding, i.e., "This is not a piece of yarn, but my nicotine addiction I bind," etc.

Tie the object into an appropriate number of knots; a single knot works well for binding a single foe, three is a good number for love, four is a number that can bring structure and confinement, seven is a good number for luck, and nine is a powerful number for binding and defense. As you tie the knots, envision the energy therein encased being twisted back on itself, bound and restricted within the form of the knot.

When your knot charm is complete, you might place it somewhere safe, carry it with you, or bury it. If you should decide you want to undo the magick, simply untie the knot to release the energies previously bound.

Points to Ponder

- Is all binding magick "bad"? Why or why not? Is binding the free will of an enemy a different cup of tea, morally, than is binding, say, your own bad habits or limiting beliefs? Why or why not?

- Just as the smugglers in the Welsh fairytale used knots in their kerchief to hold flies for later use, might a witch use a knotted string to hold an extra boost of courage or magickal charm to use when needed?

- This chapter discussed the Roma use of naturally occurring willow knots. Why do you think willow knots were seen as magickal? Could it be that just as a man-made knot can store energy, a natural knot in a willow can collect and hold a high concentration of the tree's magickal power?

- Knot charms are magickal objects that can be activated by anyone, whether or not they crafted the spell themselves. Can you think of other spell items whose magick could potentially be set into motion by a stranger? Is there a risk in using such spellcrafting techniques? Are there precautions a person could take to reduce this risk?

- If a witch is using a knot charm to restrict the actions of several powerful forces at once, is there an advantage to casting the spell into multiple knots, or would it be better to bind the energies of all these separate forces into a single knot?

If circumstances change and the witch decides to unbind just one of the several forces contained within the knot charm, would her method of releasing this individual energetic essence change depending on whether or not multiple knots or a single knot was used in the original spell?

- What particular fabrics do you think would be good to use for a knot charm to restrain the poaching of endangered animals? What color string or other material might you use in a knot charm for defense against a threatening foe?

- Might a witch use a knot charm to create a lucky talisman, using the twisted form of the knot to house desired energies chosen to attract good vibrations? What type of string or other materials would you use for such a charm?

- Could a knot charm be placed in a necktie, bracelet, necklace, shoelace, or purse string? Why might a person do so? Could a knot charm be incorporated into a hairstyle? What purposes might such a charm serve? What other applications of knot magick can you think of?

Five

Nail It Down:
Insert Magick Here

From nails pounded into binding tablets to thorns thrust into poppets, puncturing and insertion is a multi-purpose magickal technique employed in spellcrafting practices around the world, useful for binding, containing, combining, transferring, and transforming energy. In this chapter, we'll examine some traditional applications of this magickal act, and you'll learn how to apply the time-honored principles of puncturing and insertion in your own practice.

Puncturing and Insertion
Magick Around the World

One of our best known examples of puncturing and insertion magick comes to us in the form of binding tablets. Also called curse tablets or *defixiones*, from the Latin *defigere*, meaning to fix, fasten, or nail down, these magickal objects generally took the form of a sheet of lead inscribed with a curse, usually rolled up or folded and often pierced through with nails. The use of curse tablets was widespread in the Greco-Roman world for several centuries, and well over a thousand of these tablets have been found all around the Mediterranean region, with tablets dating from around 500 BCE.[59]

While not all curse tablets were punctured, the practice was nonetheless common and widespread. As these curse tablets were usually placed in hard-to-reach areas such as in wells and in graves, the nails often used to hold them together were not so much a matter of practical security as they were a matter of practical magick.[60] The act of puncturing a curse tablet with nails worked to further bind the contents of the spell, not through physical binding, but rather through a magickal binding.

One first-century tablet found in London contains seven nail holes. The tablet is not folded, and the nails were driven in from the blank side, indicating the nails had a magickal purpose rather than a utilitarian one.[61] Frequently, it seems the nails were included to add power to the curse text, which in this particular seven-holed tablet calls for the secrecy and silence of an enemy.

Some curse tablets are very elaborate, containing lengthy hexes, incantations, and symbols, while others are quite simple. The oldest examples contain only the names of the intended victims,[62] while several tablets found in France contain no writing at all.[63] Where cursing language is included

59   Gary R. Varner, *The History and Use of Amulets, Charms, and Talismans* (Raleigh, NC: Lulu.com, 2008), 36–37.

60   John G. Gager, ed., *Curse Tablets and Binding Spells from the Ancient World* (New York: Oxford University Press, 1992), 18–19.

61   College of New Rochelle, "Companion: Defixiones (Curse Tablets)," accessed March 1, 2012, http://www2.cnr.edu/home/araia/defixiones.html.

62   Daniel Ogden, "Binding Spells: Curse Tablets and Voodoo Dolls in the Greek and Roman Worlds," in *Witchcraft and Magic in Europe, Volume 2: Ancient Greece and Rome,* edited by Bengt Ankarloo and Stuart Clark (Philadelphia: University of Pennsylvania Press, 1999), 6.

63   Gager, ed., *Curse Tablets,* 34.

in the tablets, we find words demanding binding, restriction, constraint, and control, while in other tablets the binding and restricting seems to be carried out primarily through the physical binding of the tablet itself—by folding, rolling, and/or *puncturing* it.

Multi-layered magick was carried out in both the creation and activation of the curse tablets, and puncturing was but one possible element commonly employed. The act of pounding nails into the tablets worked to further "fix" and constrain the target of the spell, adding power to the spoken incantations, written inscriptions, invocations, rituals, and other elements already incorporated into the design and implementation of the curse tablet. Even the choice of materials for both tablet and puncturing nail may have been infused with magickal intent. Lead, for instance, while not the sole material chosen for the creation of curse tablets, was indeed a quite common selection for reasons both practical and magickal. Lead was a readily available material, very malleable and practical for inscribing and rolling, but it also had a magickal signature that made it a desirable medium for a binding spell. The nature of lead is cold and rather dull, making it well suited for a spell meant to induce a restriction or "freeze" of some sort. One third-century tablet states that, "Just as this lead is useless, so too may the words and deeds of those listed here be useless," while another proclaims that their victims shall become "as cold and useless as the lead."[64] The nails used to puncture and bind curse tablets were also selected for reasons both practical and magickal. Nails were typically made of iron or bronze, two common, readily available materials associated also with strength or defense. Some magicians would go through great lengths to obtain nails of a greater rarity and thus a greater power or malignancy, collecting nails from shipwrecks, coffins, and even crucifixions. As such nails were believed

---

64   Daniel Ogden, "Binding Spells: Curse Tablets and Voodoo Dolls in the Greek and Roman Worlds," in *Witchcraft and Magic in Europe, Volume 2: Ancient Greece and Rome,* edited by Bengt Ankarloo and Stuart Clark (Philadelphia: University of Pennsylvania Press, 1999), 12.

to have a connection to death and the underworld, they were considered especially potent. [65]

Sometimes, nails were incorporated in objects used in conjunction with the binding tablet itself. For example, one fourth-century Greek formula for a binding spell intended to force love called for the binding tablet to be accompanied by two clay figures, one representing the person for whom the spell is performed and the other representing the desired lover to be attracted. The figure representing the desired lover is pierced with thirteen copper needles—one in the top of the head, two in the soles of the feet, two in the ears, two in the eyes, one in the mouth, two in the stomach, two in the hands, and one between the legs. While this was done, the spellcaster would recite magickal words describing the act of puncturing: "I pierce the (whatever part of so and so) so that she may remember no one but me alone, (so and so)." [66]

Just as is the case with the curse tablets, the puncturing of the clay image here is an act of sympathetic, imitative magick, mimicking a desired effect of constraining, controlling, and restricting.

The puncturing of clay effigies as a magickal technique was also employed by the Scottish. In Donald A. Mackenzie's 1917 work *Myths of Crete and Pre-Hellenic Europe*, the author describes an act of sympathetic image magick performed by the Scottish Highlanders, involving the puncturing of a doll with sharp objects:

> *The Scottish Highland corp chreadh (clay body) was an image of an individual whom the maker desired to afflict or slay magically. Pins*

---

65   Daniel Ogden, "Binding Spells: Curse Tablets and Voodoo Dolls in the Greek and Roman Worlds," in *Witchcraft and Magic in Europe, Volume 2: Ancient Greece and Rome,* edited by Bengt Ankarloo and Stuart Clark (Philadelphia: University of Pennsylvania Press, 1999), 14.

66   John G. Gager, ed., *Curse Tablets and Binding Spells from the Ancient World* (New York: Oxford University Press, 1992), 95.

or nails were stuck into it so that the victim might suffer pain, and it
was placed in running water so that he might "waste away." [67]

Here, we again see that the insertion of the pins or nails operates on principles of sympathetic magick: a sharp object inserted in the doll is assumed to cause sharp pains in the person whom that doll represents. We see also the mention of running water being used to "erode" the victim, and in this mention an advantage of puncturing is highlighted. While the running water causes the whole body of the victim to "waste away," the insertion of a pin or nail can be done precisely, affecting concentrated areas of specific interest to the intention of the spell.

Practitioners of Brujería, a form of nature-based witchcraft originating in Mexico, also made rather shadowy use of puncturing and insertion in their rituals. An article written in 1939 relates the following method of cursing an enemy:

A method of laying spells used at San Pablito is as follows: A doll
is made to represent the intended victim. In the body little stones
taken from the river are inserted and made fast with wax. A pin
is stuck in the neck, and a splinter of orange wood in the head.
The doll is then either thrown into the river or buried in the
victim's field or in the sacred hill behind the village. [68]

We can see in this method many similarities to the Scottish method of making a *corp chreadh*. In both cases, we find that pins are stuck into an image fashioned to represent the unfortunate individual targeted by the spell. Further, we find that both methods recommend throwing the cursed doll into water, though in the Brujería method, burying is also a recommended option. Another interesting feature we find in the Brujería

---

67   Donald A. Mackenzie, *Myths of Crete and Pre-Hellenic Europe* (1917; repr., Whitefish, MT: Kessinger Publishing, 2004), 53.

68   Rodney Gallop, "A Pagan Cult Survives in Mexico," *Discovery: A Popular Journal of Knowledge, New Series,* Vol. 2, No. 10 (1939): 226–227.

method is the inclusion of stones within the mock body, inserted much like a thorn or pin in an imitative act intended to further plant undesirable energies within the enemy.

In Mecklenburg, a region of northern Germany, puncturing and insertion were also used sympathetically, and it was believed that driving a nail into a person's footprint would render them unable to walk. A similar belief was common among indigenous people of southeastern Australia, where sharp bits of bone, charcoal, glass, and quartz were inserted into the impressions made by a resting body of an enemy in order to cause arthritis and other complaints. [69]

We find the same principles of sympathetic puncturing magick at play also in the once common folk practice of sticking pins or nails into a piece of fruit or animal heart charmed to symbolize the heart of the living human victim. In *The Evil Eye: An Account of this Ancient and Widespread Superstition*, Frederick Thomas Elworthy quotes a letter written by a J. L.W. Page, dated October 20, 1890. The letter describes the discovery of a sheep's heart stuck full of pins in an old kitchen in the courthouse at East Quantoxhead, in England. Elworthy reports that animal hearts filled with pins or thorns were a common charm used to defend against witches and witchcraft throughout England. He connects the English practice with an Italian practice that appears very similar, writing about an 1892 discovery of a green lemon stuck full of nails, found on top of a valence board above a window in a home in Naples, Italy. It was a common charm in Italy; so common, in fact, that it had a special name—the *fattura della morte*, or "deathmaker." [70] Such magick works sympathetically. By charming the fruit or heart to symbolize the victim, the imitative act of puncturing is thus conveyed and transferred to the magickal victim the fruit or heart represents.

---

69   Sir James George Frazer, *The Golden Bough* (1922; repr., New York: Bartleby. com, 2000), Chapter 3, Section 3, "Contagious Magic," accessed January 9, 2012, http://www.bartleby.com/196/.

70   Frederick Thomas Elworthy, *The Evil Eye: An Account of this Ancient and Widespread Superstition* (London: J. Murray, 1895), 53–58, accessed February 15, 2012, http://www.sacred-texts.com/evil/tee/tee04.htm.

A further example of puncturing magick comes to us by way of an old Roma charm. In his 1891 work *Gypsy Sorcery and Fortune Telling*, Charles Godfrey Leland recounts a charm used to punish a faithless lover:

The deceived maid lights a candle at midnight
and pricks it several times with a needle, saying:—
"Pchâgerâv momely
Pchâgera tre vodyi!"
"Thrice the candle's broke by me
Thrice thy heart shall broken be!" [71]

These examples are pretty straightforward: puncture the tablet, puncture the figurine, puncture the footprint, puncture the candle, and the flesh-and-blood man or contrary idea or institution whom the object or footprint represents will likewise experience a similarly injurious effect. This is sympathetic magick in its most basic, straightforward, and simplest form.

However, puncturing and insertion aren't always applied for clearly sympathetic purposes. Sometimes, the techniques are employed instead to cause a transformation or transference of energy. In *Tom Tit Tot*, an 1898 work by Edward Clodd, an old English charm to get rid of a wart is thus described:

In Suffolk and other parts of these islands, a common remedy for
warts is to secretly pierce a snail or 'dodman with a gooseberry-
bush thorn, rub the snail on the wart, and then bury it, so that,
as it decays the wart may wither away. [72, 73]

---

71   Charles Godfrey Leland, *Gypsy Sorcery and Fortune Telling* (London: T. Fisher Unwin, 1891), 120, accessed January 2, 2012, http://www.sacred -texts.com/pag/gsft/gsft09.htm.

72   Edward Clodd, *Tom Tit Tot* (London: Duckworth and Company, 1898), "Magic Through Tangible Things," accessed March 23, 2013, http://www .sacred-texts.com/neu//celt/ttt/ttt08.htm.

73   This archaic formula is included for purposes of discussion only; please do not harm any animals in the making of your magick!

Here, the puncturing of the snail with the gooseberry thorn is used as a way to insert the healing properties of the gooseberry into the snail, which then keeps these healing properties when it later "becomes" the wart, having been rubbed across the affected part of the body. Through the act of puncturing, the energy of the gooseberry thorn is first transferred into the snail, mixing with its energies to transform it into a fitting ingredient for a healing spell. If the action of piercing the snail with the gooseberry thorn was carried out as a purely sympathetic action, meant to injure the symbolic stand-in for the wart, it seems more likely that the puncturing with the thorn would occur *after* the snail had been rubbed on the wart rather than before. By puncturing the snail before it ever makes contact with the wart, the snail is infused with qualities that make it easier to heal or to "transfer" the blemish. The primary object of the puncturing action here seems to be the transformation of the snail rather than the injuring of the wart. If the action of puncturing *is* meant purely sympathetically, as a way to injure the wart by injuring the snail that comes to represent it, we can gather that puncturing and insertion can have a retroactive effect. The snail is punctured before it becomes a representative of the wart itself, yet the puncturing still has its intended effect once the snail is rubbed on the wart and the transference of energy from wart to snail is complete.

We see the transference principle at play in other acts of ultimately sympathetic puncturing and insertion magick, as well; take a look at the Malay love spell below and note how the jasmine, with its love-bringing properties, is incorporated:

> … *take a lime, pierce it with the midrib of a fallen coconut palm, leaving one finger's length sticking out on either side whereby to hang the lime. Hang it up with thread of seven colours, leaving the thread also hanging loose an inch below the lime. Take seven sharpened midribs and stick them into the lime, leaving two fingers' length projecting. The sticking of the midrib into the lime is to symbolise piercing the heart and liver and life and soul and gall of the beloved.*

Put jasmine on the end of the midrib skewers. Do this first on
Monday night, for three nights, and then on Friday night. Imagine
you pierce the girl's heart as you pierce the lime.[74]

We see in this example that in addition to the sympathetic action of piercing the "heart," i.e., the lime, with the midribs, there is also an act of magickal transference and transformation going on, the energy of the jasmine mixing with the energies of the midribs, which then combine with the energies of the lime, and in turn, affect the energies of the target of the magick spell. Here, puncturing is used to transfer, combine, and transform just as much as it is used to affect a sympathetic piercing of the lime made heart. Our witchy intuition naturally surmises that without the jasmine, or perhaps with a more baneful sort of herb such as cayenne pepper, the charm would have an entirely different effect. The attributes of the jasmine, a gentle, peaceful, sensual herb, make the midribs used in the spell appropriate for the love-inducing magick at hand. Without it, the sympathetic action of piercing the lime could have a much more malignant outcome.

Hinduism is prevalent among the Malay, and in an incantation for love found in the *Atharvaveda*, an important Hindu magickal and spiritual text dating from around the twelfth to the tenth centuries BCE, we find further insight into the use of puncturing to obtain love:

May love, the disquieter, disquiet thee; do not hold out upon thy
bed. With the terrible arrow of Kama I pierce thee in the heart!
The arrow winged with longing, barbed with love, whose shaft
is undeviating desire, with that well-aimed Kama shall pierce thee
in the heart!

---

74   R. O. Winstedt, *Shaman, Saiva and Sufi: A Study of the Evolution of Malay Magic* (Glasgow, UK: The University Press, 1925), Chapter IV, "The Malay Charm," accessed March 9, 2012, http://www.sacred-texts.com /sha/sss/sss06.htm.

With that well-aimed arrow of Kama which parches the spleen, whose plume flies forward, which burns up, do I pierce thee in the heart!

Consumed by burning ardour, with parched mouth, come to me woman, pliant, thy pride laid aside, mine alone, speaking sweetly and to me devoted!

I drive thee with a goad from thy mother and thy father, so that thou shalt be in my power, shalt come up to my wish!

All her thoughts do ye, O Mitra and Varuna, drive out of her. Then having deprived her of her will put her into my power alone.[75]

The incantation was to be accompanied by a ritual in which the heart of a clay effigy was pierced with an arrow made with a thorn and an owl feather, shot from a bow with a hemp string.[76] We find here in the puncturing of the effigy the use of straightforward, sympathetic magick: just as the image is pierced and constrained by the arrow, so too is the target of the spell constrained, "deprived of her will" and put entirely under the power of the magician.

In the use of the owl feather and the hemp string, however, we find traces of something else going on, as well. Owls were associated with the Hindu goddess Lakshmi, a gentle and loving goddess believed to preside over fortune, luck, victory, beauty, spiritual wealth, material prosperity, and other auspicious aims,[77] while hemp was associated with the god Shiva, a supreme

75   Maurice Bloomfield, trans., *Hymns of the Atharva-Veda: Sacred Books of the East, Vol. 42* (Oxford: Oxford University Press, 1897), III, 25, "Charm to Arouse the Passionate Love of a Woman," accessed March 28, 2012, http://www.sacred-texts.com/hin/sbe42/av119.htm.

76   Winstedt, *op. cit.*

77   Judika Illes, *Encyclopedia of Spirits* (New York: Harper Collins Publishers, 2009), 611–612.

deity connected with transformation, healing, and purity.[78] The choice of materials used in this formula provides a positive tone for the spell, adding a layer of luck and good fortune with which to further transform the affections of the one desired. Just as in Suffolk where a gooseberry thorn transfers healing energy into a snail, here too we see elements of transference and transformation incorporated into the magickal act of puncturing. Perhaps the jasmine used to anoint the coconut palm midribs in the Malay lime charm acts in a similar manner, to simulate an "arrow winged with longing, barbed with love," able to transform the lime-made heart of the beloved through the sympathetic action of piercing as well as through the transference of the jasmine into the lime.

Common Threads and New Perspectives

In this chapter, we've examined how puncturing and insertion can be used to restrict, bind, harm, combine, transfer, and transform, and we've learned that one advantage of this technique is that it can be applied very precisely and acutely, delivering the desired dose of magick to exactly the right spot. To the modern witch, this magick might sound rather sinister, but the thing is, ugly or not, the techniques work. As a more enlightened witch of today, you can use similar techniques in good ways, positive ways, to combat major evils of the world, to help end suffering around the planet, or to help you achieve other worthy goals. Open your mind to the positive possibilities, and don't be afraid to peer into the shadows now and then to find the light.

Before we take a look at some modern applications for puncturing and insertion magick, let's review the principles underlying the techniques and discuss also a few tips that can help make your puncturing spells more potent. We've seen through our varied examples how puncturing and

---

78   Christian Rätsch, *Marijuana Medicine: A World Tour of the Healing and Visionary Powers of Cannabis* (1998; repr., Rochester: Inner Traditions International, 2001), 16–18.

insertion primarily operate either sympathetically through imitative or symbolic actions, or through a transference or combining of energies. When the techniques are used sympathetically, both the choice of actions and the selection of materials may play a role, though the actions will likely take a starring role. For example, if a person was attempting to stop a foe through the magickal act of nailing a doll-made mock enemy to the floor, the imitative act of nailing down the danger is at the heart of the magick, while the choice of nail is less important. The magician might very well select a nail with sympathetic attributes in mind. He or she might choose an iron nail for its strength, for instance, or perhaps use a gold-toned nail to imbue greater protection. As long as the sympathetic action in the puncturing spell is strong, well-chosen nails add a helpful, but not strictly necessary, extra punch. A witch might just as well choose a tin nail because that's what happens to be available in the toolbox at the moment. Since the spell is operating primarily through sympathetic magick, a sympathetic action will suffice just fine when ideally sympathetic materials are not available. When puncturing and insertion techniques are used instead to cause a transference or combining of energies, the choice of materials is more important. Such spells operate by introducing or inserting a specific energy into the image or other token meant to represent the specific target of the spell.

While the sympathetic action of inserting and/or puncturing still has a prominent place in the magick, ill-chosen materials can indeed wreck the spell through the pitfalls of mismatched mediums. For instance, if you wanted a warring country to become more peaceful, you might make a clay model of the nation and then insert into the image a piece of rose quartz, a stone with a very loving, contented energy. The symbolism and inherent energies of the stone are harmonious with the goal of the spell; the medium matches the intent. On the other hand, if a person were to cast such a spell using instead of rose quartz a nail from a shipwreck, the resulting magick would likely cause more chaos. Even if the energies of the shipwreck nail had been tempered and empowered to a new purpose beforehand, chaotic and baneful energies tend to linger and return.

By inserting an object with inherent attributes already in line with the spell, or an object that's void of any particular signature, a blank slate to empower as you wish, you're giving your magick a greater chance for success. Most definitely, objects with energies incongruous to the spell at hand can be transformed and adapted, but why take the chance and go through the trouble when efficacy matters? Save those tricks for your magickal training sessions, but leave them out of your puncturing and insertion magick if the spell is relying on energy combination or transference. The magick here is in the materials used and in the intent conveyed through the manipulation of those materials, and as puncturing and insertion at their most basic imitate stabbing, piercing, and other painful sensations, the sympathetic attributes of your spell components will need to be strong enough to outweigh this symbolism. Actions speak louder than words, so when you're using puncturing and insertion magick to combine, transfer, or transform, it's wise to supplement your well-chosen words with equally well-chosen spell materials. Keep these ideas in mind when considering the methods outlined below, and you'll gain a stronger sense of how these techniques might be useful in your own magickal practice:

Infiltration through Insertion Spell

Infiltration through insertion is a magickal technique you can use for getting you where you want to be. Want acceptance into an inner circle, or secret society? Craft an emblem out of clay to represent the group you'd like to be a part of, then write your name on a toothpick or flower stem and stick this into the clay. Alternatively, you might make a mini mock you out of clay and use that for the spell in place of the toothpick or flower stem. Want to break into show business? Draw your likeness on a pushpin and poke it into a map of Hollywood. Wish you could be at the beach? Create a twig man representative of yourself and insert it into a pot of sand enchanted to symbolize the beach of choice. Simply craft a representation of the entity or place you'd like to infiltrate, then custom-craft a toothpick, twig, or similar skewer to represent yourself. Use this barb to pierce through the image of where you want to be. You might even use the infiltration through insertion principle to help baby sea turtles reach the sea, placing a tiny model of a baby turtle within the mini-ocean of a cup of salted water.

Infiltration through insertion can also be used to bring about change and transformation. For instance, if you wanted to get some toxic coworkers to chill out, you might empower a piece of sage with a peaceful, diplomatic energy, and use this to sympathetically infiltrate an image representative of the violent regime. Want more confidence in your dealings with others? Charge up a ball of clay to represent yourself, then anoint a citrine crystal, jade stone, or oak twig with a confidence-inducing oil such as frankincense or cinnamon. Insert this into the clay to infuse your daily actions with confidence.

Sticking It to the Man Curse

Through the magickal act of puncturing, you can really "stick it to the man," so to speak. Not just for undoing personal enemies, puncturing is a technique useful for taking on larger foes, as well. Whatever your political persuasion, there are a few things we can likely agree on. Hunger sucks. Oppression sucks. Needless violence against the weak sucks. The continued destruction of the environment sucks. We might not agree on a single political solution to these problems, but as witches, we can agree that using our magick to fight such ills could help. Give it a go—cast a traditional curse upon one of the major banes of humanity and see if it works. With the puncturing technique, the process is simple and straightforward. Create an image (a clay doll, a drawing, etc.) to represent the thing you wish to get rid of, be it poverty, hate, HIV, domestic violence, or whatever other evil you want destroyed. Choose a sharp nail, a piece of iron, or an especially wicked-looking thorn to do the dirty work—stick it into the image deep, affirming that just as the barb pokes holes in the image, so too will the evil that image represents begin to break down and fall apart.

Points to Ponder

- In this chapter, we've explored some ways to use puncturing and insertion to manifest change, combat enemies, and get you where you want to be. What other applications of puncturing and insertion can you think of?

- In addition to twigs, needles, pins, thorns, nails, toothpicks, and flower stems, what other types of barbs might you use for puncturing and insertion magick? Could using different types of wood or metal make a difference in the magick? What oils or herbs might you use to enhance a puncturing or insertion spell for love? How about for a defensive spell?

- Principles of sympathetic magick, combining magick, and containing magick provide a strong basis for puncturing and insertion techniques. On what other principles might such spells operate?

- How might a person with a passion for sewing or cross-stitch incorporate a little puncturing and insertion magick into their hobby? How might a tattooist or henna artist apply these magickal techniques in their craft? Could something as simple as stirring a pot of soup or cutting a loaf of bread be transformed into an act of puncturing or insertion magick? How might a witch do so, and what purposes could such a magickal action serve?

SIX

Naming Names: Identification in the Magickal Arts

One tool for magickal accuracy that we seem to be losing in our practices is the art of naming the target. In magickal practices of the past in cultures far and wide, the importance placed on effectively identifying the point of focus in a spell is apparent. A name, a mother's name, a place of origin, an energetic signature provided in the form of hair or nail clippings—these are the tricks up the sleeve that can give a magician power and sway over gods and enemies alike. While these techniques can certainly be applied toward dark ends, the same methods can be easily adapted to help the modern spellcaster achieve magickal success for aims in line with personal ethics. Understanding and using magickal identification is an asset to the witch, whatever his or her dark or light persuasions may be. It makes spellwork more precise by telling the magick exactly where to go, who or what to affect. The magickal "target" or focus of a spell need not be a specific person. It can be a place, a thing, an idea, an ill of society. By learning some tricks for making a more precise, specific, and magickally effective identification of just where a spell should go, the magician is able to give their chances for accuracy a boost. In this chapter, we'll examine some of the tried-and-true techniques used to effectively identify the target of a spell, and you'll discover how using such methods can help ensure the success of the magick.

Magickal Identification Around the World

One way spell workers around the world have identified their magickal targets is through the very straightforward approach of incorporating the name of the person, place, or thing to be affected into the magick. Curse tablets, we have seen, often listed the name of the victim, with some early tablets consisting of nothing more than a list of names.[79] In Celtic culture also, knowing the name of the spell target was an important aspect of magickal procedure. In *The Religion of the Ancient Celts* by John Arnott MacCulloch, the following account of a curse-casting method performed by the guardian priestess of a well is given:

> *She wrote the name of the victim in a book, receiving a gift at the same time. A pin was dropped into the well in the name of the victim, and through it and through knowledge of his name, the spirit of the well acted upon him to his hurt.*[80]

We find here that power lies in the written name as well as in the symbolically named pin-made-victim. In using a combination of magickal identification techniques, the priestess helped ensure that the spirit of the well got the message.

---

79   Daniel Ogden, "Binding Spells: Curse Tablets and Voodoo Dolls in the Greek and Roman Worlds," in *Witchcraft and Magic in Europe, Volume 2: Ancient Greece and Rome,* edited by Bengt Ankarloo and Stuart Clark (Philadelphia, PA: University of Pennsylvania Press, 1999), 6.

80   John Arnott MacCulloch, *The Religion of the Ancient Celts* (1911; repr., Charleston, SC: BiblioBazaar, LLC, 2006), 196.

One point common to many magickal identification techniques around the world is the use of the mother's name. In Jewish, Greek, Arabic, and many other magickal traditions, identification of the target of the spell by their maternal lineage was standard and widespread.[81]

Using the mother's name rather than the father's name makes sense magickally because it provides a more positive identification of the intended target. While paternity is not always certain, maternity is difficult to pawn off on another; by identifying magickal targets with their mother's name, there can be no case of mistaken identities.

A sample of text from a binding tablet dating from fourth-century Rome provides an example of maternal identification in the magickal arts:

> ... this impious and ill-fated Cardelus, whom his mother
> Fulgentia bore, bound, tied up and restrained, Cardelus whom
> his mother Fulgentia bore ... [82]

In this example, we see poor Cardelus's mother identified by name in addition to her son. The magickian who crafted this tablet made certain in doing so that the spell would affect the right man, and would therefore have a better chance for success.

The practice of maternal identification, while not as well-known or as common as it once was, is still found today among magick workers around the world. In modern-day Egypt, for example, the mother's name is still used in many types of protective rituals and healing rites such as the Zar ceremony, an exorcistic healing ritual intended to relieve patients afflicted with mental disorders. In a 2010 essay by Fayza Haikal, Professor of Egyptology at the

---

81   Joshua Trachtenberg, *Jewish Magic and Superstition* (New York: Behrman's Jewish Book House, 1939), 115–116, accessed January 11, 2012. http://www.sacred-texts.com/jud/jms/jms11.htm.

82   Daniel Ogden, *Magic, Witchcraft, and Ghosts in the Greek and Roman Worlds: A Sourcebook* (New York: Oxford University Press, 2002), 212.

American University in Cairo, the importance of positive identification of the patient through the use of the mother's name is emphasized:

> ... *today when exorcism is performed during Zar ceremonies, or when protective incantations known as roqia are pronounced over children usually, but also over adults, to protect them against evil eyes ... these performances cannot be effective unless the person intended is identified by his/her name and that of his/her mother.* [83]

Parental identification was employed in ancient Egypt, as well. An ancient Egyptian magickal rite found in *The Pyramid Texts* also makes use of parental identification:

> *Utterance 293.*
> *To say: Back, hidden serpent; hide thyself,*
> *and let N. not see thee.*
> *Back, hidden serpent; hide thyself,*
> *and come not to the place where N. is,*
> *lest he pronounce against thee that name of thine,*
> *Nmi son of Nmi.t.*
> *A servant (holy person) as the Ennead's pelican (once)*
> *fell into the Nile, (so) flee, flee.*
> *Serpent (beast), lie down.* [84]

Here, we have a positive assertion that one's name holds power—the magician here threatens the "serpent," promising to "pronounce against thee

---

83   Fayza Haikal, "The Mother's Heart, the Hidden Name, and True Identity: Paternal/Maternal Descent and Gender Dichotomy," in *Echoes of Eternity: Studies Presented to Gaballa Aly Gaballa,* edited by Ola El-Aguizy and Mohamed Sherif Ali (Wiesbaden, DE: Otto Harrassowitz Verlag, 2010), 197.

84   Samuel A. B. Mercer, trans., *The Pyramid Texts* (New York, London, Toronto: Longmans, Green, and Co., 1952), Utterance 293, accessed January 1, 2013, http://www.sacred-texts.com/egy/pyt/pyt14.htm.

that name of thine, Nmi son of Nmi.t.,"[85] lest the "serpent" hide itself and not come 'round. The text implies that if such a name were pronounced, the "serpent" would be in some way harmed or otherwise controlled. We have here therefore an expression of the idea that knowing a person's or god's identity, knowing their parental lineage, gives a magician power and sway over that person or god.

To the Finnish, knowing the origin and history of an enemy, in addition to knowing their parental lineage, provided an important means of magickal identification and establishing dominance. John Abercromby's 1898 work *Magic Songs of the West Finns, Vol. 2*, offers an example of the technique in action. Check out this spell used to combat an enemy:

> *O wasp, the stinging bird, O gadfly, bubbling o'er with wrath, O*
> *hornet, thou complaisant man, don't shoot thine arrows forth*
> *into that human skin, that body of a mother's son. Surely I know*
> *thine origin, together with thy bringing up; thou wast conceived*
> *by Synnytär, brought up by Kasvatar. Blind was thy father, blind*
> *thy mother, thou art blind thyself. In the snow thy father died, in*
> *the snow thy mother died, in the snow thyself wilt die.*[86]

The phrase "Surely I know thine origin" helps establish the magician as dominant over this foe, able to will it to die in the snow like its mother and father. In this example, we see also that the simple assertion that one knows the lineage, history, and origin of the enemy is enough to take power over

---

85   "Nmi" and "Nmi.t" are translated as "traveler" and "female traveler," respectively, according to Wim van den Dungen's article at sofiatopia. org titled, "The Pyramid Texts of Unas: The Royal Ritual of Rebirth and Illumination," accessed January 1, 2013, http://maat.sofiatopia.org /wenis_text.htm#XII.

86   John Abercromby, *Magic Songs of the West Finns, Vol. 2* (London: David Nutt, 1898), 108, accessed January 3, 2013, http://www.sacred-texts.com /neu/ms2/ms204.htm.

that foe. The magickian refers to the enemy as "conceived by Synnytär, brought up by Kasvatar," and makes further claims as to the vision and place of death of these "parents." Synnytär was a personification of birth, while Kasvatar was a personification of growth. These are not literal parents, and it's doubtful that the utterer of these words actually knows "thine origin" and "thy bringing up" of the "wasp" here accused, and yet the phrases seem to have supposed magickal power, nonetheless. By using metaphoric, figurative language, the Finnish magician was able to bolster their claim to knowledge regarding the foe's identity, and was thus able to obtain power and control over the menacing and stinging "wasp."

Identification through a name or an origin isn't only useful for battling foes and other misfortunes; it's a practice useful in coercing deities, as well. An early Egyptian text establishes the utterer as an equal to the gods, and one of the "credentials" mentioned is knowing the names of those gods:

> *HAIL, thou lotus! Thou type of the god Nefer-Temu!*
> *I am the man that knoweth you, and I know your*
> *names among those of the gods, the lords*
> *of the under-world, and I am one of you.*
> *Grant ye that I may see the gods who are the*
> *divine guides in the underworld, and grant ye unto me*
> *a place in the underworld near unto the lords of Amentet.*
> *Let me arrive at a habitation in the land of Tchesert,*
> *and receive me, O all ye gods, in the presence of the lords of*
> *eternity! Grant that my soul may come forth whithersoever it*
> *pleaseth, and let it not be driven away from the presence of the*
> *great company of the gods!* [87]

---

87   Marah Ellis Ryan, *Pagan Prayers* (Chicago: A.C. McClurg and Company, 1913), "Prayer of Transformation into a Lotus," accessed March 23, 2013, http://www.sacred-texts.com/pag/ppr/ppr14.htm.

Here, the utterer states, "I am the man that knoweth you, and I know your names among those of the gods, the lords of the under-world, and I am one of you." By knowing the names of the gods, a certain kinship is established, a form of proof given to show one's worth to have a "place in the underworld near unto the lords of Amentet" and to "not be driven away from the presence of the great company of the gods!"

Another interesting example from Egypt illustrates that the names used to identify the gods need not be proper nor flattering. Identifying an entity by a false, impolite, or slang name can have power as well, just as identifying an entity by their real name has a magickal effect. Mercer's translation of *The Pyramid Texts* lists the following incantation as a protection placed on a pyramid enclosure; included here is a brief excerpt from the original text:

> ... *If Nephthys comes in this her evil coming; that which is said to her is this her name of "substitute without vulva ..."* [88]

Here, instructions are given to the enclosure that if the goddess Nephthys should attempt to breach the pyramid with ill intentions, she should be called "substitute without vulva." This title don't seem very nice when you consider it's being applied to a deity. In Egyptian myth, Osiris was tricked by Nephthys into sleeping with her rather than with his beloved Isis, who was the sister of Nephthys and her complete opposite. Where Isis represented life and fertility, Nephthys represented barrenness and death. [89] The rather rude-sounding moniker of, "substitute without vulva," highlights the less pleasant or more unusual qualities of Nephthys in an attempt to prevent her from rendering harm upon the dead. In calling the goddess out on her indiscretions and idiosyncracies, power over the divine is obtained. Perhaps

---

88   Samuel A. B. Mercer, trans., *The Pyramid Texts* (New York, London, Toronto: Longmans, Green, and Co., 1952), Utterance 534, accessed January 1, 2013, http://www.sacred-texts.com/egy/pyt/pyt29.htm.

89   Ancient Egypt Online, "Nephthys," accessed March 13, 2013, http://ancientegyptonline.co.uk/nephthys.html.

it's true that we can never escape our wrongdoings, and the least attractive qualities we possess are as sure a way to identify us as is our name and parental lineage.

Another technique of magickal identification to note is the use of physical elements to supply the energetic signature of the spell target. Hair, nail clippings, and other body-derived ingredients are commonly used to identify the focal point of the magick, and when these are not available, a written or verbal description of the person's physical traits, or a photograph of them, are often employed. If the focus of a spell is a place or a thing rather than a person, the modern witch might use drawings, photographs, dirt or stones from a particular locale, a bit of gold to symbolize a heap of gold, or other means to capture the energetic essence of the magickal target.

Common Threads and New Perspectives

Now that you know how magicians of the past have identified their spell targets using names, parental lineage, idiosyncrasies, origin, physical traits, and even metaphor, consider ways you might apply these techniques in your own modern practice. Might knowing (or even pretending to know!) the origin of the bad luck you've been having offer you some measure of ability to send that bad luck packing? Could failing to be precise in identifying the target of a love spell have unexpected consequences? When magick fails to reach its intended target, the spell may still have effects, only unplanned and elsewhere. Positively identifying the spell target helps ensure that your magick goes exactly where you want it to go, diminishing the risk of ineffective and/or misdirected magick.

Magickal Identification in Practice

Magickal identification need not be applied only when it comes to the main focus or "target" of the spell. Identifying other spell components as specifically as possible does much to boost the efficacy of the magick. Just as the full name, parental lineage, place of origin, physical traits, and idiosyncrasies of an enemy or other magickal target can be useful in controlling and directing the magick, so too does incorporating identifying characteristics of the power sources used in the spell help call into action the specific forces and energies needed to make it happen.

Such power sources include, for one, yourself, the spellcaster. Unless it's a rather sneaky spell you'd rather not take cosmic credit for, refer to yourself by name, magickal name, maternal lineage, place of origin, idiosyncracies, physical traits, metaphoric or figurative language—as many identifying aspects as you feel comfortable sharing with the other "power sources" aiding you in the magick. These other sources of power might include deities, spirits, stones, plants, fellow witches—anything else that lends its energy or aid to the magick at hand.

Be as specific as possible in your magickal identification. If you know the proper name of a thing, by all means, use it. Ditto with origin and parental lineage. If you know not origin nor lineage nor proper name, use general identifying language that could be true of nearly anyone, i.e., "son of the mother who bore him." Remember, figurative language and metaphor can be used where knowledge is lacking, also. For example, if you were casting a spell for protection against an unknown yet venomous enemy who seemed to appear out of nowhere, you might identify this foe as, "the snake who hid in the shadows," or, "the snake who crept up from under the rock," or something similar. Idiosyncrasies can be useful as well, but are more of an extra layer of specificity rather than a primary means of identification. Especially where solid knowledge about proper name and background lacks, information about idiosyncrasies is indispensable in filling the gaps. Let's take a look at some examples to better illustrate how this all might pan out in actual magickal practice.

Best Case Scenario

In our hypothetical "best case scenario," you know the full name and history of the person to be affected by the magick. You know their parental lineage and their place of origin. You know their idiosyncrasies, and you even have a photo and a piece of their hair to give your magick spell an extra boost. Your spell might make use of as many of these identifying characteristics as possible. Your magickal identification might sound something like "Mary Carter, born July 1st, 1979, daughter of Rebecca Carter, Mary Carter who lives at 391 Elm Street in Topeka, Kansas, Mary Carter who was born in Savannah, Georgia, who has red hair, who stands 5' 7" tall, who wears glasses, who bites her nails, who drags her feet, who has a squeaky voice." In addition, the photo and the hair would be incorporated, perhaps laid on the altar as a point of focus or added to a lucky talisman or protective amulet.

Similarly, if a place rather than a person is to be the focus of a spell, history, location, and physical or geographical features can be used to help establish identity. For example, if I were doing a spell to protect the town I live in, I might refer to, "Denver, Colorado, founded in 1858, Denver in the midwestern US, Denver with mountains to the west and plains to the east." A photo or postcard depicting the town, as well as a stone or some soil taken from the place might also add strength to the connection and power to the magick.

An object might likewise be identified by its history, location, and physical features. If you were empowering a new wand, for example, you might identify the wand as, "this wand that I hold in my hand, this wand that was born from the oak tree, this wand that was carved with the knife, this wand that is twisted and bent," or similar.

Some Advantage

Let's take a look at another hypothetical situation, imagining this time that we have only limited information regarding the focus of our spell. Suppose, for instance, that we want to do some magick to protect homeless dogs in our area. We don't know what these particular dogs look like, we don't know their names or origins, and we don't know their precise location. We only know that we have a whole bunch of dogs in our city that we'd like to protect. In this "limited information" scenario, the witch would play up what they *do* know, and make use of generalities, imagination, guessed idiosyncrasies, and figurative language to fill in the blanks. For example, our unknown homeless dogs might be identified as "the homeless dogs that live outside in Atlanta, the dogs who sleep under trees, who sleep in the alleys in Atlanta, the brown dogs, the white dogs, the black dogs, the multi-colored dogs, the dogs with short hair, the dogs with long hair, the dogs with curly hair and fluffy hair, the puppy of a mother dog, the dog who's searching for a light in the storm, the dog with a drooping tail, the dog who wanders, lost," or some such lengthy and detailed outline describing exactly *which* dogs we are aiming to help. Even if our descriptions are very general, there is power in the specifying itself, helping to concentrate and direct our magickal power to exactly where it's needed most.

Likewise, if your spell is focused on an unknown place, generalities, imagination, and metaphor can pick up where factual information stops. For example, if you wanted to perform a spell to help capture a fugitive on the loose, your magick might center around sealing off, "that ground on which the fugitive now stands, the earth beneath the fugitive's feet, that place that is a trap for the beast, the town that is a prison for the fugitive, the place whose air the fugitive now breaths, the place whose sights the fugitive now sees, the place whose perimeter is now sealed."

If the focus of your spell is a physical object that is far away, very large, or otherwise unattainable, try using a smaller "model" of the original as a means of magickal identification. For example, if you're working a spell to protect a large marble building in another part of the country from where you live, try using a small piece of marble to forge a link of identification with the true, full-scale target of the magick.

In the Dark

Now suppose you know next to nothing about the person or place to be the focus of a spell. In establishing magickal identification in such a case, generalities, imagination, and metaphor will here be invaluable. For example, suppose you're aiming to attract to yourself your ideal love match. You feel certain you've yet to encounter this person, and thus have no idea what they look like, how they act, or where they live, much less their name and who their parents are. In this case, you might make the magickal identification with generalities such as "the one whose spirit matches mine," or "the one who loves me passionately and unconditionally."

You can use imagination and figurative language to help prop up and better define these general descriptions. Delve into your innermost fantasies and see what you come up with, see what you sense. Then use this intuitive knowledge to help identify your mystery partner. For example, you might describe your dream lover as "the one whose eyes are like a dark starry night, the one whose skin is like the warm, strong earth, the one who sees me as an equal, the one who *is* my equal, the one who holds me close to the tree, the master who calls me darling," or any other such name that speaks to your most deeply held desires and most persistent intuitive instincts. Be as specific as possible; the greatest benefit of magickal identification is that it narrows down the options for where a spell might choose to land.

Points to Ponder

- Do you believe that there is power in a name? If so, what is the nature of this power?

- How much of a god or a man does a name encompass? What aspects of one's true identity are reflected in a name? Which aspects are not?

- Having a magickal name or a secret name can be a handy tool for self-protection as well as for powerful magick. By having a name no one else knows, the power of that name is reserved for you and your gods alone, and no one can use it against you. What are some additional benefits to having a hidden name?

- In addition to the use of names and parental lineage, this chapter also discussed origin as a means of magickal identification. In what ways do our actual or metaphoric roots connect us with who we are in the present moment? Do you think that in knowing the beginning of a thing, that therein lies the power to potentially destroy (or create) it?

- Body-derived ingredients such as hair, fingernails, or saliva can be useful in the magickal identification of a particular person, just as soil, stones, and flora can help establish the energetic identity of a specific locale. What other types of substances might be useful in magickal identification?

- Can you think of any additional methods of magickal identification not discussed in this chapter?

seven

Decoy Magick

The decoy principle is a magickal theory that can be effectively applied for cursebreaking, curse prevention, spell diversion, and spell recall. It's the idea that a curse or other spell can be diverted away from its original target by using a decoy to create a distraction and take the heat of the magick. The decoy principle is particularly useful in its scope and versatility, as it can be employed to not only break active curses, but also to prevent them or divert them before the ill intentions have a chance to reach their target. In addition, the decoy principle can also be effectively applied in situations where a love spell or other less malicious but still unwanted magickal intention has been hurled your way. The decoy principle can even be used to affect our own magick, offering us a way to "call back" or otherwise divert spells we've cast before having a change of heart that makes the earlier magick undesirable or obsolete. In this chapter, we'll examine some of the many ways the decoy principle has been applied in different cultures, different times, and different places, then we'll see how these same ideas can be expanded to suit the modern witch.

Decoy Magick Around the World

One example of the decoy principle in action is probably already familiar to you; in fact, you might have such a decoy buried in your yard right now; its use still common in England, America, and elsewhere. The witch's bottle is used to render protection through the means of diversion. Although construction methods vary, generally the object consists of a bottle or flask filled with a mixture of blood, urine, saliva, hair, nail clippings, rusty nails, pins, thorns, and other unsavory objects. The bottle is then buried or hidden in or near the home to draw off and absorb any curses or other ill intentions directed toward the house's occupants.

More than two hundred witch's bottles dating from the sixteenth and seventeenth centuries have been unearthed to date, with a majority of the bottles containing some combination of iron and human-derived materials such as urine, blood, hair, and fingernails. According to an article in *Current Archeology*, one witch's bottle discovered in a ruined cottage just south of London was analyzed by a Dr. Alan Massey, and it was found to contain traces of urine, hair, and bent pins. The iron often incorporated in the bottles frequently takes the form of nails or pins that have been bent into an L-shape.[90]

Here, the human-derived ingredients provide the energetic similarity with the intended victim needed to make the bottle into a proper decoy that will attract the curse. The hair, urine, blood, or fingernails provide the energetic signature of the would-be victim, thereby creating a vibrational similarity that "tricks" the curse into entering the bottle rather than affecting the originally intended person. The bent pins or nails, thorns, or other sharp objects are included as a way to further divert, confuse, harm, or damage the curse once the ill-wrought magick reaches its psuedo-target.

The African Wanika, a large tribe centered in the Coastal Province of what is now southern Kenya, also made use of the decoy principle. In *Religion*

90   Dr. Alan Massey, "The Reigate Witch Bottle," *Current Archeology*, no. 169 (2000): 34–36.

and Myth, an anthropological study published in 1883, James Macdonald describes how the Wanika might perform an exorcism ritual to expel an evil spirit from a victim. The Wanika believed that illness was caused by malicious spirits, and in order to heal the sickness, the evil entity had to be brought out and away from the patient. To start the rite, drums are played wildly, and other loud, raucous noises are made in order to help distract and excite the demon. A brightly colored stick decorated with beads and other trinkets is placed in the ground to further attract the demon's attentions away from the victim. The people play like they are having a good time, partying and playing music, in order to trick the evil spirit into believing that they have let their guard down. The spirit eventually becomes enthralled with the colorful stick and is enticed by its dazzling appeal to enter into it. The magician leading the exorcism then pulls the stick out of the ground, thereby trapping the demon within it. [91]

In this example, the music, the mock revelry, and the lavishly decorated stick combine into an enticing distraction that lures the negative spirit away from the victim. Once the evil entity lets its guard down, it's guided into the stick-made-decoy and captured, leaving the patient free from further harm.

In addition to enticement and distraction, confusion can also be employed in decoy magick. In an early twentieth century annual report from the Bureau of American Ethnology, Walter E. Roth writes about a practice of the Carib tribe of South America, describing how they use a string puzzle to confuse and waylay unfriendly spirits. The Carib string puzzle consists of two flat pieces of wood connected with a seemingly endless, winding string. When used for entertainment, the object of the game is to remove the string without untying any knots or making any cuts. The string puzzles aren't just used by children, however. The Carib, if lost, might place one of these string puzzles in the middle of the path, believing that the spirit who

---

91   James Macdonald, *Religion and Myth* (London: David Nutt; New York: Scribner, 1883), 104–105, accessed May 5, 2012, http://www.sacred-texts.com/afr/ram/ram08.htm.

is leading them astray will be distracted and enthralled by the challenging plaything, leaving the wanderer to continue on to the right path. Roth also mentions a similar practice witnessed in the lower Amazon regions, where a young boy braided a palm leaf, formed it into a ring, and hung it on a branch in the path for the purpose of confusing and thwarting any potentially dangerous or misleading spirits.[92] The winding string on the string puzzle, and the twisted plaits on the palm leaf ring, serve a common purpose. The winding, twisting formations provide a complex path to traverse, thereby distracting and confusing any unfriendly spirits and diverting these energies away from their intended course.

Yet another example of decoy magick for spirit diversion might be found in the widespread practice of throwing stones toward grave sites in order to repel any unfortunate souls who might otherwise attempt to leave their grave and follow. From the Pennsylvania Germans in America to the Baganda tribe in Eastern Africa, the practice of pelting stones and other missiles at graves believed to be inhabited by the restless dead is a long-standing tradition. In an 1889 issue of the *Journal of American Folklore*, W. J. Hoffman, MD, reports that the Pennsylvania Germans made it common practice to throw stones when passing by the burial sites of suicides and other victims of violent death, as well as places where bodies were buried on unconsecrated or otherwise unsavory ground. Failing to do so was believed to put oneself in danger, as a restless ghost might give chase if not diverted.[93]

---

92   Walter E. Roth, "An Inquiry into the Animism and Folk-lore of the Guiana Indians," in *The Thirtieth Annual Report of the Bureau of American Ethnology, 1908–1909* (Washington, D.C.: 1915), Chapter VIII, "The Spirits of the Bush," section 109, "Why the Drink Turned Sour," accessed June 1, 2012, http://www.sacred-texts.com/nam/sa/aflg/aflg08.htm.

93   W. J. Hoffman, MD, "Folk-Lore of the Pennsylvania Germans, Part II," *Journal of American Folk-Lore*, 2:4 (1889): 31, accessed May 5, 2012, http://www.sacred-texts.com/ame/fpg/fpg02.htm.

Far away in Baganda, a landlocked country in eastern Africa, the practice was very much the same. In his 1928 work *The Vampire: His Kith and Kin*, Montague Summers cites an excerpt from *The Baganda*, a 1911 work written by Reverend J. Roscoe, which reports that the Baganda tribe had a practice of pelting the ground with sticks and clumps of dirt when passing by places where the bodies of suicide victims had been burned. Behind the practice was a belief that this action would prevent the ghosts from following, just as the Pennsylvania Germans reasoned when throwing stones at graves.[94]

The practice was common in Madagascar and in southern Africa as well. Summers cites also an 1875 work by Fr. Finaz, S. J., published in *Les Missions Catholiques, vii*, in which Fr. Finaz offers accounts of the Marave, a tribe in southern Africa, throwing stones when walking past places where "witches" and other unfortunates had been burned. At some of these locations, large mounds of stones piled up over time, and Fr. Finaz conjectures that the Marave believed that the spirits might eventually become thoroughly trapped by these growing mounds of stones.[95]

In these various examples, we see the primary purpose of the stones, the clods of dirt, the sticks being the same—to momentarily distract any potentially lingering ghosts for long enough to allow the passerby to pass by unnoticed, without attracting attention and without provoking attack. Alternatively, it might be surmised that these missiles serve instead the purpose of "physically" harming the corporeal form of the ghosts, but this seems unlikely for several reasons. If the stones and sticks and dirt were meant to actually harm the invisible bodies of the restless spirits, it seems the people would attack these hostile spirit-inhabited areas a little more

94   Montague Summers, *The Vampire: His Kith and Kin* (London: K. Paul Trench, Trubner, 1928), 148, accessed February 14, 2013, http://www.sacred-texts.com/goth/vkk/vkk05.htm.

95   *Ibid.*, 328, accessed February 14, 2013, http://www.sacred-texts.com/goth/vkk/vkk07.htm.

seriously, with their best weaponry and with the combined force of many warriors, not with individuals flinging mere clumps of earth. Also, if the cairn of stones that might arise on such spots is intended as a physical barrier that can indeed eventually keep an angry spirit in its grave, why wouldn't the people simply pile up the rocks from the get-go, right after the body is burned or buried? Another thing to consider is that the grave sites are most likely already full of naturally occurring sticks and stones and earth. If these objects are on their own enough to harm or trap a ghost, why must they be handled and thrown in order to do the trick?

It seems rather that the magick here is in the decoy. The personal energy that becomes imparted to the stones or clumps of earth when they are handled and then tossed by random passersby is enough to distract the ghost so that the innocent traveler can successfully sneak past. The handling forges the energetic similarity between decoy stone and real-life passerby that tricks the spirit into heading for the false target; without that energetic similarity, the stone is no more than a stone.

Another widespread example of the decoy principle in action is the use of eye beads. The beads are typically made of glass, ceramic, wood, bone, or gemstones and fashioned to resemble the human eye. In Asia, the Middle East, the Americas, and elsewhere, it's believed that wearing such an amulet confers immunity against the evil eye and other dangers. Eye beads made their first appearance in western Asia, Egypt, and India, but their use eventually spread throughout much of Europe and beyond.[96] In *The Illustrated Bead Bible: Terms, Tips, and Techniques*, the author describes the use of eye beads as amulets to guard against the evil eye:

> *The protective strategy is to distract the evil eye by making it look first at something other than your eye. The bead features a symbolic*

---

96   "Nazar Boncugu or Turkish Evil Eye Bead Amulets," accessed March 11, 2013, http://www.nazarboncugu.com/.

eye—a circle, dot, or natural shape like a cowrie shell—that is carved, molded, painted, or embedded into its surface. [97]

Here, the decoy works not through energetic similarity derived from contact or the inclusion of hair, blood, etc.; instead, the eye bead decoy relies on an energetic similarity acquired through sympathetic attributes. Just as a heart-shaped leaf can attract love since its appearance forges a sympathetic connection to the human heart, so too does an eye bead operate by looking like an eye. The sympathetic attributes shared by representations of the eye, and the actual eyes of the would-be victims, provide for an energetic similarity between the two. This allows the eye amulets or eye beads to act as decoys to distract and attract any ill intentions that would otherwise be cast towards the real eyes of the would-be victim.

In ancient Egypt, decoy magick was employed in a practice involving animal sacrifice. Just as was the case with eye beads, here also were sympathetic attributes at the heart of the magickal distraction. According to Elworthy's *The Evil Eye: An Account of this Ancient and Widespread Superstition*, the Egyptians managed to bypass certain requirements to sacrifice humans by substituting animal sacrifices, instead. Elworthy writes that these unfortunate animals were marked with a seal bearing the image of a man, hands bound and kneeling, a sword held at his throat.[98] This use of imagery creates a false sympathy between decoy animal and real-deal human sacrifice, and the newly created energetic similarity that results is enough to convert the animal into an effective substitute. Fortunately, we don't go around sacrificing animals or humans for magickal purposes these days, but this same method of using imagery to create a false sympathy is still a valid technique in modern decoy magick.

---

97   Theresa Flores Geary, PhD, *The Illustrated Bead Bible: Terms, Tips, and Techniques* (New York: Sterling Publishing Co., Inc., 2008), 115.

98   Frederick Thomas Elworthy, *The Evil Eye: An Account of this Ancient and Widespread Superstition* (London: J. Murray, 1895), 82, accessed February 15, 2012, http://www.sacred-texts.com/evil/tee/tee04.htm.

Common Threads and New Perspectives

From the various examples in this chapter, we learn that decoy magick takes many forms, and that it can operate through a variety of magickal mechanisms. Decoys can function through enticement and distraction, as in the Wanika exorcism, through confusion, as in the example of the Carib string puzzle, or through energetic similarity with the intended target, as is the case with both the witch's bottle and the eye beads. These aren't the only ways in which a decoy can do its work, of course, but they're indeed tried-and-true methods that can be used to veer a spirit or spell off-course in a flash. Let's take a closer look at how each of these principles might be applied.

Confusion

Confusion is a technique used often in decoy magick, its purpose being to distract, engage, and ultimately contain or lead astray an undesirable spirit or spell. In the examples of the Carib string puzzle and the Amazonian boy's braided palm leaves, we find the confusion rendered through the twisting, winding formations wrought into the design of the decoy objects. Just as jumbled and snaking writing might be employed in a binding tablet in order to diminish and constrain a foe, so too does the twisting, braiding, and looping sometimes incorporated into the physical form of a decoy object act to guide both spirits and magickal energies away from their intended destinations. As if stuck in a maze, the energy becomes disoriented and confused by the labyrinth structure and is forced to forgo its original course. In addition to winding, twisting shapes, jumbled sounds, masquerade, and a little raucous activity can also be useful in creating confusion.

Enticement

Sometimes all that's needed to break a curse or banish a bad spirit is a little temptation. Useful in recalling spells both before and after they hit their mark, enticement can be an effective decoy that will distract both spirits and magickal energies away from current pursuits. In the example of the

Wanika tribe's exorcism ritual, music, dance, revelry, and the lavishly and colorfully decorated stick are irresistible to the offending spirit, and it's tempted out of the body of the victim and into the stick where it's trapped.

When using enticement to employ the decoy principle, you'll need to think about the types of energy that might distract and attract the particular magick you are hoping to thwart or undo, then decide how you can incorporate those characteristics into the decoy to make it undeniably tempting.

Here are a few ideas to consider for inspiration:

For Mischievous Energies and Spirits

When you're dealing with a spirit or magickal energy of a mischievous or playful nature, try using music, games, charade, bright colors, and movement as enticement. These whimsical, fun, and dazzling elements will distract the magickal energy and tempt it to leave its post and enter the decoy. Confusion is also effective against mischievous energies and spirits, and it can be used in conjunction with enticement to great result.

For Greedy Energies and Spirits

For spirits and energies of a greedy nature, shiny objects or other symbols of wealth and power work well. Use coins, blades, blood, or other similar enticements to lure away the unwanted magick.

For Malicious and Hateful Energies and Spirits

When you're aiming to thwart a truly malicious and hateful energy or spirit, it's emotion you want to impart to the decoy. Fill the decoy with love, spiritual brightness, compassion, or even feigned despair. Rub tears on it. Laugh into it. Empower it with sheer emotion. Through these or similar methods, the decoy can become infused with enough "life energy" to tempt the baneful energy into attacking it. Once the distraction has been made and a new target—the decoy—takes the brunt of the spell or curse, the original victim is freed from further harassment.

For Generally Pleasant Energies and Spirits

When trying to break a spell or ditch an energy or spirit that is generally not unpleasant, you'll want to use similarly pleasant energies and elements in your decoy construction. Try incorporating energies similar to the energy or goal of the original spell. For example, suppose you've cast a spell to attract a new lover, only to decide a few days later that what you really need is some time to yourself. Instead of having to fend off all the would-be suitors that are likely to come your way, you can instead use the decoy principle to recall, or retract, your original spell post-cast. You would need to find a way to make the decoy appealing to the energy of the love spell, perhaps imbuing it with attributes that make it appear like a suitable courtier, or by simply infusing it with energies of love and passion. Loving energies distract and attract loving energies; a friendly ghost who has become a bit too friendly is enticed away by energies reminiscent of their own previous life. By attuning your decoy with the energy you are hoping to distract, the decoy becomes an attractive and tempting target through the principle of like attracting like.

Energetic Similarity

When you're using the decoy principle to divert or prevent unwanted magick before it strikes, crafting a decoy that relies on energetic similarity is a solid option. Here, the decoy acts as a stand-in, or substitute, for the person that would otherwise be the target of the magick. In the example of the witch's bottle, we see the decoy principle being applied in this fashion. Complete with hair, urine, and other human components, the bottle-turned-decoy object has an energetic similarity with the would-be victim that makes it appear to actually *be* the would-be victim, which confuses the curse into striking the bottle as if it has found its true target.

Energy knows energy, and when a curse hits a properly prepared decoy, it thinks it has hit its mark and that its work is done, which, of course, effectively prevents the curse from doing its intended damage upon the correct target of the magick. Here we see one of the special advantages of using energetic similarity to craft a decoy—the curse is "fooled" into acting as if it has reached its intended goal, and the curse-caster who might be checking up on his or her spell's progress is likely to intuit the same diagnosis of success, and thinking the work is done, might back away from attempting any further damage.

Take care in planning and preparing a decoy that relies on energetic similarity. You don't want the decoy to be too representative of the "actual" target—if you do so, it might strengthen rather than weaken the unwanted magick's ability to take affect. The key is to give the decoy enough similarity so that its energy mimics the energy of the would-be target, but to hold back from too strongly connecting the would-be target's energy to the energy of the decoy.

If you wanted to create a decoy to act as a stand-in for yourself, for instance, you would infuse the decoy with the basic energetic life force you project to other people—with an energy that mimics the most outer, surface you. This is enough to cause the decoy to appear to be enough like you that the curse or other unwanted magick will find it and be "fooled." If the association is made too strongly, however, the energies of the decoy object can become attached to your own energies, making the decoy object not so much a substitute for you, but rather an actual symbol of you. Curses and other spells will easily travel on that connection and go from symbol you to real you with little or no hesitation.

This distinction between symbol and substitute is essential when crafting a decoy based on energetic similarity, so let's examine it more precisely. When making a symbol, the intentions and visualizations are directed with the idea of the object becoming a representation of the larger idea it encompasses—a small poppet becomes a mini-you, for instance; a pentacle becomes the wealth or protection it calls to mind. Here, the connections are drawn deeply enough that the core energies of the symbol become attached to the core energies of whatever the symbol symbolizes. In contrast, when you are creating a substitute, the substitute is connected to the "genuine article" only through surface energies, not through the innermost, most real and unique essences that make the fake a fake and the real deal the real deal.

In creating a substitute, you only want to create a facade upon the object—think of it as putting a "you" costume on the decoy object. The decoy object does not become you, and it does not symbolize you. It is not connected to your core being in any way. Just like using baking powder instead of baking soda in a recipe, the decoy simply substitutes and takes your place. When we are substituting in magick, for instance, using rosemary rather than rose petals in a love spell, the rosemary does not in any way become a symbol of the rose petals—it is another thing entirely, but its energies are similar enough to the rose petals that it will have a similar effect in your spellwork. When you are substituting a decoy for yourself in order to prevent a curse or divert a spell before it strikes, the decoy is acting as the rosemary standing in for rose petals—the decoy simply takes your place, but it in no way becomes you.

In contrast, if you *did* want to create a symbol of yourself, you would want to actually name the object as such and think about it in those terms. You would sense the innermost energies of yourself and of the symbolic object, and you would consciously weave and join these energies together to form a bond. The object then becomes a symbol of you, a representation of you that is exacting and detailed enough that its energies are literally connected to you. Can you anticipate the problems that might arise if you were to accidentally use a symbol rather than a substitute when applying the decoy principle for spell diversion and curse prevention?

Creating a substitute rather than a symbol isn't as tricky as it sounds, and there are many ways to prepare a decoy to an adequate extent without going overboard. Forging an energetic similarity between the decoy object and the person to be protected does take finesse, but that finesse is more in the mental process than in the method. As we've seen from the examples in this chapter, there are several very simple and effective ways to impart energetic similarity to a decoy. Let's take a quick look at these, then we'll discuss how to actually put this decoy magick into action.

Handling

Handling the decoy is one very easy, very quick way to impart energetic similarity. Through direct contact and touch—through the contagion principle or the principle of close proximity, in other words—the decoy is imprinted with the energetic essence of the person to be protected and is thus effectively converted into an adequate substitute. This is the method employed in the stone-throwing practices discussed earlier in this chapter. If you'd like to try the technique yourself, don't over think it. You might simply hold the object momentarily, rub it briefly, or otherwise put it into contact with your body. Think only about your outermost surface energies "rubbing off" on the object, creating a substitute rather than a symbol of you. This is enough to impart your energy and "fool" the curse or other spell, but not enough to literally connect you with the decoy in potentially unfortunate ways.

Human-derived Ingredients

Another method you might use to create a similar energetic essence in the decoy object is to include personal ingredients like hair, urine, nail clippings, or saliva—just as is done in the construction of a witch's bottle. When using such ingredients, you don't need to do anything extra to empower them or impart intention—they are already strongly imprinted with your energy, and extraneous handling can risk imparting on the ingredients a symbolic quality that will directly connect you to the decoy.

Sympathetic Connection

Sympathetic connections are also a way to achieve energetic similarity in a decoy. In sympathetic magick theory, objects that share similar physical characteristics also share similar energetic characteristics—the star, or pentacle, in the cross-cut apple core becomes associated with wealth; thorny briars become associated with pain and curses. The eye beads discussed earlier in this chapter are a prime example of a decoy that gains its energetic similarity through sympathetic connection.

By choosing a decoy that already has a sympathetic connection to the person or place to be protected, much of your work in forging an energetic similarity is already done. For instance, if you're tall, slender, and bubbly, a Barbie doll who has the same hair color as you could be a ready-made decoy to divert and absorb any spells cast your way. Likewise, if you were aiming to protect an animal, a plush toy that looks similar could be an adequate substitute. Keep in mind that a sympathetic connection doesn't have to be natural. It can be consciously fashioned and created, just as the ancient Egyptians forged their own sympathetic connection between animal sacrifice and human sacrifice through the simple medium of adorning the animal's body with an image of the human.

Decoy Magick Spells

As you can see, decoy magick is as varied and diverse as it is powerful. It can be used for curse breaking, curse prevention, spell diversion, spell recall, general protection, and more. It can work through enticement, confusion, or energetic similarity acquired through handling, sympathetic attributes, or human-derived ingredients. Your decoy object might be as simple as a stone picked up from the ground and held momentarily, or it can be as complex as a carefully designed, handcrafted poppet that looks just like you. Let the urgency and purpose of the decoy guide the design, and keep in mind the difference between substitutes and symbols as you craft your magick—you'll want a substitute, not a symbol, and to accomplish that you need only to keep front and center in your awareness the fact that you are pulling a trick on the unwanted magick.

Below are a few techniques to illustrate some of the possible applications of decoy magick. Choose a method according to the general need, and adapt to suit.

Proactive Decoy Magick

Decoy magick can be used proactively, to divert and thwart spirits, spells, and curses alike before they find their way to your doorstep. Such decoys can be used for general protection, spell diversion, spirit diversion, or curse prevention. Since pro-active decoy magick is meant to work in an ongoing and protective fashion, crafting a decoy object that can be kept around for a while is a good choice. Consider incorporating energetic similarity into the design of the decoy, and be sure to empower it with your intentions before use. Envision the decoy doing its work, absorbing the energies it aims to divert. If you like, say something such as, "This is your target. Go here; go here." Once activated, simply place the decoy object near the person or place to be protected. You might want to keep the decoy someplace hidden, or you might choose to craft a very normal-looking decoy out of an every-day object that you can leave out in plain sight without rousing the slightest suspicion. Check the decoy object every now and then to make sure it's still intact and that its energies feel fresh and active. If it seems damaged or dull in any way, destroy it and craft a new one.

Decoy Magick for Spell Recall

To use decoy magick to call back or divert a spell post-cast, you'll need to first locate the magickal energy you're aiming to distract. Unless the spell you want to undo is attached to a specific object or location, this part can be a bit tricky. Try to decipher as much as you can about the originally cast magick; if it's your own spell you're recalling, you've got this one in the bag because you'll already know everything about it. If it's another person's spell, use what you know about their typical methods to make your best guesses. Make use of items, symbols, or ingredients known to have been used or likely to have been used in the original spell. For example, if you suspect the original spellcaster used either plants or stones in their magickal act, refer directly to both the spell "cast with plants" and to the spell "cast with stones" in order to give yourself the best shot at correctly identifying and thus gaining the attention of the original magick. Likewise, if it's your own spell you're breaking and you know for a fact you cast it with a candle, place the same candle on your altar to summon back the original spell. You might use words, symbols, and actions from the original spell also. Simply imitate what you know or suspect of the original spellcasting, then use new words, intentions, and the action of the decoy magick to reverse, twist, or undo the unwanted charm. This act of similarity forges a connection to the original casting that reverts the spell back to an earlier, more malleable stage of the magickal process where it can be more easily deflected and deterred. Elements of confusion or enticement can also be incorporated. Once the original magick has been located or summoned back through imitative words, ingredients, items, symbols, or actions, use confusion or enticement as a decoy to steer the energy in a new direction. Keep in mind that a decoy doesn't need to be an object, nor does it need to be solely one thing—it might be a dance, a song, a bit of theatrics, or any other form of tempting or disorienting distraction.

Decoy Magick for Cursebreaking

If you're using decoy magick to free a person from a curse, within and around the curse victim is where you will find the offending energy. Directly call out the baneful vibration; implore the ill-wrought magickal energy to take notice and pay attention. Once the energy to be thwarted has been summoned to the forefront, use decoy magick to distract and tempt it. When working with strong or very negative energies, using an actual object for the decoy is beneficial as doing so provides a more solid, stable structure with which to attract and hold the original magick. Use enticement or confusion to do the trick. Wave the decoy object around, light candles around it, ring bells—anything you can think of to draw attention towards the decoy. Think of the curse or other unwanted magickal energy that you are hoping to deflect, and envision these energies exiting the victim and going straight into the decoy object, bypassing all else without notice.

Be aware of the energies present. When you sense the unwanted energy has entered the decoy object or has otherwise turned away from its original target, remove the newly freed curse victim or spell target from the area. If the energy has entered a physical decoy object, stamp the object on the ground, bury it, or break it to prevent the energy from escaping back to its original host. Beat drums, ring bells, or clap loudly to further drive away any lingering offending energies.

Points to Ponder

- This chapter presented several examples of decoy magick from around the world, including the exorcism ritual of the Wanika tribe and the witch's bottle used in England, America, and elsewhere. Do you agree that these practices could be described as decoy magick? Why or why not? How else might such techniques be classified?

- What other examples of the decoy principle in action can you identify? Have you ever used such techniques in your own practice?

- Have you ever been in a situation where employing decoy magick for curse prevention, curse breaking, spell diversion, or spell recall could have been beneficial? How might you have crafted such magick?

- This chapter offered several methods for constructing a decoy using energetic similarity, including handling, using sympathetic attributes, and including body-derived ingredients like hair or urine. Can you think of any other ways a decoy could be made energetically similar to a person? How might a decoy that shares an energetic similarity with a place be constructed?

- We discussed how decoys can operate through energetic similarity with the intended target, through enticement and temptation, and through confusion. What other foundations of decoy design can you think of?

- The decoy principle offers a way to veer magick off-course. Do you agree that the effects and actions of spells can, and sometimes should, be altered post-cast? What reasons might a witch have for doing so?

- Have you ever cast a spell that didn't work as you expected, that perhaps affected something other than its originally intended target? Might the decoy principle have been at work?

- This chapter discussed the use of body-derived ingredients to provide the energetic similarity required for certain types of decoy magick. How does this differ from the use of such ingredients for the purpose of magickal identification? *Is* there a difference? If so, is the difference in the method, or in the mental process?

- Could the decoy principle be employed to help prevent needless worry? Could it possibly be used to aid in disguising one's appearance? What other creative applications of the decoy principle can you think of, and how might such magick be accomplished?

- Could it be said that a decoy attracts energy as much as it diverts it? Why or why not? Instead of using a decoy to divert and ward off negative magick cast your way, could a decoy be used instead to actually attract positive energies? Why or why not?

- Is the power and purpose of a decoy more in the design or in the intent? Why do you think so?

Eight

Cursebreaking and Countercharms: Magick to Undo

Though the infamy of cursing has given us sorcerer types a bad rep, much of the magick humanity has cast throughout the ages has been defensive and healing in nature, meant to counteract and ward off both present and potential dangers, curses, threats, and injuries. Not nearly as much attention has been given to the methods used to *undo* a curse as to the methods used to *cast* a curse, which is a shame considering most modern witches agree, it's much better to heal than to harm. Decoy magick, we have seen, is one technique that can be used for cursebreaking, but it's by no means the only technique. In this chapter, we'll take a look at a sampling of other methods magicians around the world have employed to break curses, neutralize spells, and otherwise defend themselves against both magickal and mundane attacks.

Cursebreaking and Countercharms Around the World

Hair of the Dog

Just as body-derived ingredients can play a role in decoy magick, so too can they act as key elements in other forms of defensive spellwork and cursebreaking. In 1940, the Georgia Writer's Project published *Drums and Shadows*, a collection of folklore assembled from interviews conducted during the 1930s with elderly African-Americans living in the coastal areas of Georgia. Many of the interviewees had been slaves, and their magickal practices were directly reflective of older various African beliefs and techniques. One of the essays in the collection interviews Nathaniel John Lewis, mayor and resident of Tin City, a very small, very impoverished settlement to the east of Savannah, Georgia. He explains how a person in his community might counteract an act of conjure:

> "… *cunjuh must be fought with cunjuh. If I know my enemy's name I could get somethin frum a cunjuh doctuh to help me seek revenge.*
>
> … *The toe nails, the finguh nails, even the scrapins frum the bottom of the foot are all very powuhful. If the doctuh could get any of these frum my enemy, he would mix them in whiskey an make my enemy drink.*" [99, 100]

Here, we again find the assertion that body-derived ingredients such as toenails, fingernails, and skin can be used to combat negative magick; in this case, however, it's ingredients derived from the body of the *enemy*

---

99   Georgia Writer's Project, Savannah Unit, Mary Granger, District Supervisor, *Drums and Shadows* (Athens, GA: University of Georgia Press, 1940), "Tin City," 12, accessed May 15, 2012, http://www.sacred-texts.com/afr/das/das07.htm.

100   The phoenetic dialect spelling used in the original text is preserved here also to provide an accurate transcription of the oral testamonies offered by the interviewees and to bring these stories back to life in the voices with which they were originally told.

that does the trick. In contrast to the witch's bottle, which defensively employs as a decoy body-derived ingredients originating from the people to be protected, here we find the curser's own bodily substances used offensively against their own person. As if the act of casting a curse leaves its mark within our very flesh, the curser's skin, toenails, and fingernails have turned toxic. Karma shows her hand, and the body-born, energetic signature of the curser proves to be their own undoing. One wonders if such a charm would work equally well on the innocent.

In other cursebreaking formulas, we find ingredients derived from the body of the curser acting as a medicine for the afflicted rather than as a poison to the guilty. In Texas along the Rio Grande, one countercharm used against *el ojo*—the evil eye—employed the curser's saliva as a key ingredient. In her 1923 essay highlighting the Mexican influence on local folk beliefs, Florence Johnson Scott described a common *remedio*—or cure—for the curse of el ojo. The procedure began by cracking an egg over the head of the victim. If the evil eye curse was indeed at work, a small eye would become visible in the egg yolk. Whenever this happened, a search for the person responsible for casting el ojo would begin. It was believed that the curser would be sure to have a terrible headache, and in this way, the guilty party would soon be discovered. The offender was then brought before the sick person, where he or she was expected to administer the cure:

> *The offender found, he must go to the sick person, take a mouthful of water, and from his own mouth transfer it into the mouth of his victim. This remedio is supposed to effect instantaneous cure, but if it does not, there are other prescribed treatments. In each and all of them, however, the offender takes the place of the nurse.*[101]

---

101   Florence Johnson Scott, "Customs and Superstitions among Texas Mexicans on the Rio Grande Border," in *Coffee in the Gourd*, edited by J. Frank Dobie (Austin, TX: Texas Folklore Society, 1923), section IV, "Omens and Superstitions," accessed February 1, 2012. http://www .sacred-texts.com/ame/cig/cig14.htm.

The transference of the water from the mouth of the curser to the mouth of the victim would surely transfer also a good dose of the curser's saliva. Here, the bane becomes the balm and the ingredients derived from the body of the curser provide a magickal healing. The act of eating a part of something else imitates having complete power over that something else; by ingesting someone's saliva, the power inherent in that saliva becomes your own (along with all their germs, too). Since the saliva here would contain the energetic signature of the curse, consuming it becomes an act of imitative magick that consumes the curse, as well. There is also an element of mixing magick going on here. As the curser's saliva mixes with that of the victim, the energies combine, transforming and diluting the magick of the original curse.

In New England also were body-derived ingredients employed to break curses, though here the ingredients were derived from the body of the victim rather than from the body of the curse-caster. In *The Salem Witch Trials Reader*, Francis Hill includes an excerpt from Chadwick Hansen's book *Witchcraft at Salem* describing a popular method of cursebreaking:

> *One of the commonest countercharms for a bewitched animal was to cut a piece off of it—frequently an ear—and burn it or boil it… This kind of countercharm verged on black magic because it was supposed not only to break the witch's spell but to injure the witch or compel her presence. It could be used with people as well as with animals, although you did not, of course, cut off the person's ear. You cut some of their hair or took some of their urine, and boiled it.* [102, 103]

---

102   Chadwick Hansen, excerpt from *Witchcraft at Salem* (New York: G. Braziller, 1969), in *The Salem Witch Trials Reader,* edited by Francis Hill (Cambridge, MA: Da Capo Press, 2000), 245.

103   This is another example of an archaic method included here for discussion and historical interest; please do not cut or otherwise harm animals in your magick-making.

Sometimes, nails or thorns were added to the urine, making this charm quite similar in form to that of the witch's bottle. In both recipes, we have a vessel filled with bodily fluid from the person to be protected, and we find also the inclusion of sharp objects in both formulas. The witch's bottle acts as a pro-active decoy, there to stand guard and fool any future curses into hitting the bottle rather than the witch. The witch's bottle is used most often not to break an active curse, but rather to preempt any future threats that might come into play. The urine contains the energetic signature of the person to be protected, and through the connection forged through this similarity, future curses may be decoyed and diverted. The urine boiling formula, on the other hand, is used after the fact, as a healing, defensive measure to break the spell of suffering caused by an active curse. The bodily fluids of a curse victim contain the energetic signatures of the curse and the curser as well as that of the victim; through the imitative act of heating the urine and adding sharp objects to it, the energies represented within the urine are likewise affected. The curse is broken, the curser is tormented, and the energies of the newly cured victim are purified. Of course, the witch's bottle could be utilized in this same manner, providing relief to those already under the influence of a curse. In such a scenario, the magick would be in the imitative action of physically containing the urine within the bottle, thereby containing and trapping the energies of the curse and thus isolating the infection away from the victim. While the outward form of methods may look very similar, the heart of the magick, as usual, is in the subtle difference of intent.

Destroying the Curse Object

If you're not into cutting off locks of people's hair or squirreling away toenail clippings, no worries—there are lots of other ways to counteract a curse. One method that has been widely used for cursebreaking is to destroy, or at least remove, the curse object, those material components used to cast and contain the original curse. This method only works if there *is* such an object, of course, and only then if you can find and properly dispose of said item. A resident of Sunbury, a small rural community in Georgia, described in an interview conducted in the 1930s an incident of conjure involving a curse object and its destruction. The woman relayed the story of an old man who was terribly bothered with eye problems. He dug up his yard and eventually discovered the cause of the trouble: a curse in the form of a doll, its fingers stuck in its eyes, buried right beneath the door step. The man reportedly threw the doll in a river, bringing an immediate end to both the curse and the eye trouble. Similarly, a resident of Sandfly, another nearby rural community, shared a story about a woman she knew who was able to stop a curse caused by a conjure bag:

> *A woman that lived in Homestead Park jis couldn't seem to have nothin but bad luck. She thought maybe an enemy had conjuhed uh, so she looked in the yahd an sho nough theah wuz a cunjuh bag. It wuz a queah lookin bundle with a lot of brown clay in it. She destroyed the bag an the bad luck stopped an the evil spirits didn't bothuh uh none.* [104]

We can see in these anecdotes the sheer amount of hard work and physical labor that might be involved in destroying a curse object in order to break a spell. The man and woman here mentioned must first dig around their yards until the suspicious object is found. Depending on the extent of a person's property, discovering a curse object through this method could take anywhere from ten minutes to ten months—potentially a great deal of work that could fail to yield any benefit.

Of course, there are things a person can do to help shorten the search. Divination or dowsing may be used to obtain clues to the object's whereabouts, and likely places for cursed object deposit can be checked first. Top spots to check include near thresholds and door frames, near or below gates, around the four corners of your yard or the four corners of your home's exterior, in pillows, and in mattresses.

---

104   Georgia Writer's Project, Savannah Unit, Mary Granger, District Supervisor, *Drums and Shadows* (Athens: University of Georgia Press, 1940), "Sunbury," 111, accessed May 15, 2012, http://www.sacred-texts.com/afr/das/das15.htm.

If and when a curse object *is* located, disposing of the curse is then quite simple. Destroy the conjure bag, destroy the curse; plunge the doll in the river, and drown the spell. The aim of destroying the curse object is to disrupt the energetic structure of the magick as much as possible. Effective methods include breaking, burning, burying, and sinking. Although the initial search for a curse object might be quite tedious and potentially unfruitful, if you find what you're looking for, destroying or even banishing the physical form of the magick is one of the most efficient and surefire methods of cursebreaking that a witch can use.

While it's not wise to hold back when it comes to countermagick, sometimes a curse can be dispersed by merely disturbing or relocating the object that houses the charm. Although it's certainly preferable in most situations to destroy any such token outright to prevent any further damage to others, simply moving a cursed object to a new location will certainly move the magick and alter the action of the spell, sometimes transforming, diverting, or reversing the originally cast curse. One example of breaking a curse through curse object removal comes to us from the wide world of sports. In 2008, Gino Castignoli, a diehard Red Sox fan who was hired to do construction work on the new Yankee stadium, decided to try his hand at casting a curse against the Yankees. The Yankees and the Red Sox have had a long-standing rivalry ever since the so-called "Curse of the Bambino" struck the Sox back in 1918 (more on this one later!), and Castignoli wanted to help even the score. He attempted to levy ill wishes against the Yankees by burying a Red Sox jersey beneath the new Yankee locker room. The Yankees owners were tipped off to the curse by other construction workers, and a plan was devised to foil Castignoli's magickal attempt. The Yankees organization hired workers to jackhammer and drill through two feet of solid concrete in order to locate and retrieve the cursed jersey, which was then donated to a charity auction.[105] The curse removal took five hours

---

105   Sushil Cheema, "The Big Dig: The Yanks Uncover a Red Sox Jersey," *The New York Times*, April 14, 2008, accessed January 5, 2013, http://www .nytimes.com/2008/04/14/sports/baseball/14jersey.html.

and carried a price tag of $50,000, a pretty hefty investment coming from people who most likely consider magick to be a bunch of superstitious nonsense![106] The jersey had only been buried for a week, but what happened after it was removed highlights the reality of the curse. The tattered and torn garment bore the name and number of David Ortiz, one of the star players for the Red Sox. The day of the jersey's removal from beneath the concrete was one of the worst in Ortiz's career. He just couldn't seem to get his game together and that night was pulled from the starting line-up to take a "mental break." There are two lessons here—one, that a curse once cast will strike *somewhere*, and two, that people should be careful when messing around with magick. Castignoli wanted only the Yankees to lose, but with a poorly thought-out spell design, he ended up cursing one of his favorite team's players, instead. Of course, the Yankees owners weren't too expert in their cursebreaking procedures, either, and by merely removing the jersey rather than destroying it outright, they may have allowed some of the curse's originally intended effects to linger. The Yankees failed to make the playoffs in 2008, for the first time in fifteen years.

Overpowering: Breaking a Curse through Direct Magickal Warfare

Another way to divert a curse or other unwanted energy is to fight back. By directing toward the source of the negative intentions an adequately powerful attack, the would-be curse or other misfortune can be overpowered and stopped before it has a chance to do its worst. Overpowering as a cursebreaking technique was used widely by the Maori of New Zealand. Edward Shortland's *Maori Religion and Mythology* offers us a prime example of such direct magickal warfare, explaining how the Maori magickal masters

---

106   John Usma, "Reversing the Curse: Red Sox Jersey Excavated from Yankee Stadium," COEDMagazine.com, April 14, 2008, accessed January 5, 2013, http://coedmagazine.com/2008/04/14/reversing-the-curse-red-sox-jersey-excavated-at-yankee-stadium/.

used *Whakahokitu*, a special form of *makutu*—or sorcery—designed to overcome and overpower curses cast by rival experts of the art:

> WHAKAHOKITU *is the name given to forms of makutu employed to counteract the curse of some other tohunga, or wise-man; for whoever practises makutu, even though he be skilled in the art, may have to yield to the mana of some other wise-man who can command the assistance of a more powerful Atua. The following is a specimen of this kind of makutu—*
> *Great curse, long curse,*
> *Great curse, binding curse,*
> *Binding your sacredness*
> *To the tide of destruction.*
> *Come hither, sacred spell,*
> *To be looked on by me.*
> *Cause the curser to lie low*
> *In gloomy Night, in dark Night,*
> *In the Night of ill-omen.*
> *Great wind, lasting wind,*
> *Changing wind of Rangi above.*
> *He falls. He perishes.*
> *Cause to waste away the curser tohunga.*
> *Let him bite the oven-stones.*
> *Be food for me,*
> *The tapu and the mana,*
> *Of your Atua,*
> *Of your karakia,*
> *Of your tohunga.*[107, 108]

---

107   Edward Shortland, *Maori Religion and Mythology* (London: Longmans, Green, and Co., 1882), 35, accessed February 2, 2012, http://www .sacred-texts.com/pac/mrm/mrm05.htm.

108   *Tohunga* is a Maori word meaning expert at an art or trade. *Mana* is an indwelling, impersonal force existing within all beings and in many inanimate objects as well. *Atua* is a word meaning a power, or god.

We see here that the curse is first called forth, to be "looked on" by the defending magician. He then relies on the power of his words and intentions to cast a countercurse against his enemy—whether or not this action will neutralize his rival's magick depends solely on whether or not the defending magician is more powerful than his foe. If he is the stronger, then he can use his own sorcery to overpower and counteract any magickal attacks from the weaker *tohunga*.

The energy used to overpower a curse need not be negative or malicious; evil can be fought with good just as well as it can be fought with further menace. Among Hungarians living in Transylvania, a historical region in central Romania, the task of cursebreaking is often given to the *călugăr*, a priest or monk in the Romanian Orthodox tradition of Catholicism. One cursebreaking procedure still actively used today requires the *călugăr* to recite blessings upon a photo or the clothes of the victim, while in another formula, sugar or oil is blessed and then mixed with the victim's food.[109] Both methods rely on the greater strength of the good to overpower and overcome the strength of the bad. The recited blessings, the food-turned-sacrament, the garments rendered purified—all are deemed powerful enough to override a curse and provide a cure. Here, the introduction of positive intentions transforms the magickal landscape, rendering the originally cast curse diluted and thus ineffectual.

Making Amends

As we see in the example of the *călugăr* cursebreaking rites, fire doesn't always have to be fought with fire. In fact, sometimes it's best to not fight at all, but rather make amends and make it right. Making up with the people or powers responsible for placing a curse in the first place is indeed an often

---

109   Eva Pocs, "Curse, Maleficium, Divination: Witchcraft on the Borderline of Religion and Magic," in *Witchcraft Continued: Popular Magic in Modern Europe,* edited by Willem De Blécourt and Owen Davies (Manchester: Manchester University Press, 2004), 182.

reliable and safe way to break a spell. Many of our cursebreaking methods lead only to more trouble; as the first curse is broken and a countercurse hurled, a new curse is cast to counteract the countercurse…and thus does the wizard's dual commence. By focusing instead on trying to make it right, the witch is minimizing the likelihood of courting further ire. Sure, there are principles of dignity involved, and a person might not want to simply roll over and apologize to the big bad wolf. Yet, a small sacrifice of pride is sometimes a worthy price to pay to avoid further large-scale punishment! Such tactics have certainly worked in the city of Philadelphia, where several years ago a decades-long curse was broken through the simple expedient of making amends. According to urban legend, the curse in question, nicknamed the William Penn curse, was activated way back in 1987. Before then, the city had honored Philadelphia's founding father William Penn by ensuring that the town hall, which features a William Penn statue on its roof, would remain the tallest building in the growing metropolis. Tradition was broken and the curse was set in motion with the 1987 construction of the Liberty Place building. The city's first skyscraper, the building rose far above the William Penn statue atop the town hall. Before this, the city's sports teams were among the best in the nation, with the Eagles even enjoying a trip to the 1980 Superbowl. Once William Penn was no longer the highest point in the city, however, the sports rankings started to plummet in earnest. Philadelphia teams went without a major title year after year after year—from 1987 all the way to 2008.

What eventually broke the curse was the power of a thoughtful gesture, an action taken in an attempt to make amends and make things right with the city's founding father. When the Comcast Center was erected in 2007, it became the city's new tallest building, and in an effort to cure the drought of sports wins, a 25-inch statue of William Penn was placed at the very top, high on the roof where it would once again be literally above all else in Philadelphia. Jeanne Leonard, a spokesperson for the construction company involved with the cursebreaking, explains the inclusion of the miniature William Penn:

"To reinforce that the building would lift whatever curse there is, we decided that he would take his rightful place at the top of the city again."[110]

It seems that the magick of making amends worked for Philly. In 2008, the curse of William Penn was broken when the Phillies finally won the World Series again for the first time in a long time.

In Germany relief from curses has also been obtained by making amends. An anthropological study of the folk magick practices in Franconia, an isolated province in central Germany, was conducted by Hans Sebald in the late 1970s and early 1980s. One woman provided testament of an incident of malicious witchcraft and the simple means of making it right that was used to break it. Sebald writes:

One of my case studies deals with a woman who stole from a witch-reputed neighbor. Soon thereafter she perceived a vengeance spell causing her cows to milk traces of blood. Knowing the traditional solution of Abbitte (asking to be forgiven), she visited the witch, offered restitution, and begged that the curse be lifted from her stable. The witch complied; the cows returned to normal.[111]

In this example, we find that often a curse is merely an act of karma, delivered by the witch who acts as an administrator of divine justice. Since the curse was indeed somewhat justified (the woman did steal from the witch, after all), by owning up to her mistake and offering some form of restitution,

---

110   Kevin Horan, "William Penn Atop Philly Once Again," MLB.com, October 3, 2008, accessed January 10, 2012, http://mlb.mlb.com/news/article.jsp?ymd=20081027&content_id=3648489&vkey=ps2008news&fext=.jsp&c_id=mlb.

111   Hans Sebald, "Shaman, Healer, Witch: Comparing Shamanism with Franconian Folk Magick" (1984), repr. in *Witchcraft, Healing, and Popular Diseases: New Perspectives on Witchcraft, Magic, and Demonology, Vol. 5,* edited by Brian P. Levack (New York: Routledge, 2001), 319.

the curse victim is able to make things right and prompt the witch to call back the malicious magick. It takes great bravery to stand face to face with the ones we've wronged and apologize, but doing so is often the best way to restore balance and harmony when a curse is wreaking havoc in our lives.

Reflection as a Means of Cursebreaking

Another effective way to break a curse is through the reflection principle. By creating a reflective energy surrounding the intended curse target, the curse is bounced back on its caster.

We'll explore some examples of exactly how magicians around the world have done this, but first off, let's consider the theory behind the method. A reflection reverses an image. When a person gazes into mirrored glass, their image doesn't penetrate the glass's surface. Instead, it's reflected back, and we see this mock, reversed image as our "self"—we accept it as such and we generally don't think of this image as a reversal of our true appearance. We accept the mirror's reflection as our own image. Similarly, a curse, when it finds its intentions mirrored back, will accept those effects as its own doing. The reflection principle of magick is the idea that by creating a negative, or reversed, otherwise-replica of the essential idea the original curse or spell represents, the magick can be stopped in its tracks, tricked into thinking it has already done its worst by meeting with its apparent effects manifested. The spell then returns to its place of origin, bringing the full brunt of its magickal force home to the one who cast it, just as the karmic consequences of any spells we utter flutter back to us inevitably.

The reflection principle has been applied in varied ways around the world. In Egypt, the reflective power of words was used to break curses and hurl ill intentions back to the one who sent them. An example found on the wall of an ancient pyramid does well to illustrate:

To say: "Spitting of the wall"; "Vomiting of the brick," that which
comes out of thy mouth is thrown back against thyself [112]

Carved into the west wall of the sarcophagus chamber of the Pyramid of Unas,[113] this utterance was intended to protect the tomb and its dead from malicious magick or other misfortune that could otherwise hinder the soul's journey into the afterlife.[114] We see here the directive for "that which comes out of thy mouth" to be "thrown back," and we find the very substance of the pyramid itself "spitting" and "vomiting" out any curses sent its way. By naming the energies to be diverted and then using one's words and intent to mirror and reverse those energies, the enemy's spells are counteracted, reflected back to their origin.

Reflection as a means of cursebreaking can also be found in traditional Hindu practice. In the *Atharvaveda*, many charms used to repel malicious magick make ample use of the reflection principle. Take a look at this excerpt from Hymn V, 14:

V, 14. Charm to repel sorceries or spells.
… 4. Take hold by the hand and lead away the spell back to him
that prepares it! Place it in his very presence, so that it shall slay
him that prepares the spell!
5. The spells shall take effect upon him that prepares the spells,
the curse upon him that pronounces the curse! As a chariot
with easy-going wheels, the spell shall turn back upon him that
prepares the spell!

---

112   Samuel A. B. Mercer, trans., *The Pyramid Texts* (New York, London, Toronto: Longmans, Green, and Co., 1952), Utterance 241, accessed January 1, 2013, http://www.sacred-texts.com/egy/pyt/pyt09.htm.

113   "Pyramid Texts Online," accessed January 1, 2013, http://www .pyramidtextsonline.com/.

114   The Ancient Egypt Site, "The Pyramid Complex of Unas," accessed January 1, 2013, http://www.ancient-egypt.org/index.html.

6. Whether a woman, or whether a man has prepared the spell
for evil, we lead that spell to him as a horse with the halter
… 10. Go as a son to his father, bite like an adder that has been
stepped upon. Return thou, O spell, to him that prepares the
spell, as one who overcomes his fetters!
11. As the shy deer, the antelope, goes out to the mating (buck),
thus the spell shall reach him that prepares it!
12. Straighter than an arrow may it (the spell) fly against him, O
ye heaven and earth; may that spell take hold again of him that
prepares it, as (a hunter) of his game!
13. Like fire (the spell) shall progress in the teeth of obstacles, like
water along its course! As a chariot with easy-going wheels the
spell shall turn back upon him that prepares the spell! [115]

Here again we find clear directives for the clearly identified spells of the enemy to be reflected back. Orders such as "lead away the spell back to him that prepares it," "the curse upon him that pronounces the curse," and "return thou, O spell, to him that prepares the spell" are quite clear—the same energies incorporated into the original curse are to be hurled directly back upon the curser, just as powerful, just as strong, as if they had met their intended mark. As in Egypt, so too in India was the reflective power of words and a reversal of intentions used to prevent, thwart, and break a variety of curses.

The Pennsylvania Dutch also made use of reflection magick, though their methods were quite different than those of Hindu or Egyptian magicks. In a collection of folklore gathered by John George Hohman, originally published in the nineteenth century, a technique of counteractive magick is described that highlights the unusual quality of the Pennsylvania Dutch techniques:

---

[115]   Maurice Bloomfield, *Hymns of the Atharva-Veda: Sacred Books of the East, Vol. 42* (Oxford: Oxford University Press, 1897), V, 14, "Charm to Repel Sorceries or Spells," accessed March 28, 2012, http://www.sacred -texts.com/hin/sbe42/av090.htm.

If you are calumniated or slandered to your very skin, to your very flesh, to your very bones, cast it back upon the false tongues. Take off your shirt, and turn it wrong side out, and then run your two thumbs along your body, close under the ribs, starting at the pit of the heart down to the thighs.[116]

It seems here that the efficacy of such actions is primarily in their oddity, which gives the whole operation a reversing quality. In addition, when the slanderous energies of the gossipers hits the rather backward, reversed version of their target, these energies are reflected back, just as if the gossip was looking at itself in the mirror. Whether it's mostly the oddity or mostly the mock reversal that tricks the gossip is impossible to determine. What is clear, however, is that we have here a doubly reflective, doubly reversing action that works to stop ill wishes fast, sending the malicious intentions back from whence they came with a very simple, easy-to-perform act of multi-layered reflection magick.

Other studies of cursebreaking through reflection are also challenging to define in terms of most active ingredients. One such example is the aforementioned Curse of the Bambino, one of the best-known, longest-running curses in baseball history. Legend has it that the curse was set in the off-season of 1919–1920, when the Red Sox sold star player Babe Ruth, nicknamed "the Bambino," to the Yankees. At this early point in baseball history, the Red Sox had won five of the first fifteen World Series and were expected to continue to do well. After trading Ruth, though, the team hit a downward spiral that continued for ages, with the Red Sox failing to win the World Series title time and time again. It took until 2004 for the Red Sox

---

116   John George Hohman, *Long Lost Friend* (1820; trans., Camden: Star and Book Novelty Company, 1828), "A Good Remedy Against Calumniation or Slander," accessed March 23, 2013, http://www.sacred-texts.com /ame/pow/pow009.htm.

to break the curse and once again reclaim the World Series title.[117] Credit for the curse's reversal is split. Some believe the Curse of the Bambino was broken at a game on August 31, 2004, when an especially wayward foul ball hit by Red Sox player Manny Ramirez hit a young fan in the face and knocked out two of his front teeth. Although the battered onlooker was a Red Sox fan and an avid supporter of Manny Ramirez, he had connections to Babe Ruth through the fact of living on Sudbury farm, land that was once owned by the baseball legend.[118] Sending a baseball hurtling into the face of this Red Sox fan turned Babe Ruth representative may have mirrored and thus reversed the harmful effects of the original Curse of the Bambino.

Others tout the reflective power of words as the true charm that broke the famed curse. Shortly prior to the 2004 Red Sox win, a Boston street sign warning against a "Reverse Curve" was vandalized and changed to state, instead, "Reverse the Curse."[119] The city was so wary of jinxing their home team that they left the graffiti in place until after the Red Sox had secured the World Series title. Whether it was the foul ball or the sign that did it, we'll never know, but through either a reflective word or a reversing action, reflecting a curse away from its target is a powerful and effective defense.

Using reflection as a means of countermagick and cursebreaking doesn't have to be a complicated operation. As we've seen in these examples, it can be as simple as using reflective language, reflective intent, bizarre actions. Through the reflection principle, your magick becomes a mirror to confuse,

117   Joseph Lin, "The Curse of the Bambino," October 19, 2011, in "Top 10 Sports Superstitions," Time.com, accessed January 5, 2013, http://keepingscore.blogs.time.com/2011/10/19/top-10-sports-superstitions/slide/curse-of-the-bambino/.

118   Brian McGrory, "Taking Teeth Out of Curse? Teen Hit by Ramirez Foul Ball Lives in Babe Ruth's Former House," September 2, 2004, *The Boston Globe*, on Boston.com, accessed January 5, 2013, http://www.boston.com/news/local/articles/2004/09/02/taking_teeth_out_of_curse/?page=full.

119   Dan Shaughnessy, *Reversing the Curse: Inside the 2004 Boston Red Sox* (New York: Houghton Mifflin Company, 2005), 231.

reverse, and reflect the original spell or curse so that it's sent back upon its caster.

Covering All the Bases

In addition to the widespread use of body-derived ingredients, destruction of the curse object, overpowering, and reflection as effective means of curse-breaking, another commonality apparent in countermagick practices around the world is the act of "covering all the bases," as it were, making a counter-spell more effective by increasing the chances that the nature of the original spell will be correctly guessed. An example will serve to better illustrate this principle; take a look at this countercharm offered in the *Atharvaveda*:

> V, 31. Charm to repel sorceries or spells.
> 1. The spell which they have put for thee into an unburned vessel, that which they have put into mixed grain, that which they have put into raw meat, that do I hurl back again.
> 2. The spell which they have put for thee into a cock, or that which (they have put) into a goat, into a crested animal, that which they have put into a sheep, that do I hurl back again.
> 3. The spell which they have put for thee into solipeds, into animals with teeth on both sides, that which they have put into an ass, that do I hurl back again.
> 4. The magic which they have put for thee into moveable property, or into personal possession, the spell which they have put into the field, that do I hurl back again.
> 5. The spell which evil-scheming persons have put for thee into the gârhapatya-fire, or into the housefire, that which they have put—into the house, that do I hurl back again.
> 6. The spell which they have put for thee into the assembly-hall, that which (they have put) into the gaming-place, that which they have put into the dice, that do I hurl back again.
> 7. The spell which they have put for thee into the army, that

which they have put into the arrow and the weapon, that which they have put into the drum, that do I hurl back again.

8. The spell which they have placed down for thee in the well, or have buried in the burial-ground, that which they have put into (thy) home, that do I hurl back again.

9. That which they have put for thee into human bones, that which (they have put) into the funeral fire, to the consuming, burning, flesh-eating fire do I hurl that back again.

10. By an unbeaten path he has brought it (the spell) hither, by a (beaten) path we drive it out from here. The fool in his folly has prepared (the spell) against those that are surely wise.

11. He that has undertaken it has not been able to accomplish it: he broke his foot, his toe. He, luckless, performed an auspicious act for us, that are lucky.

12. Him that fashions spells, practises magic, digs after roots, sends out curses, Indra, shall slay with his mighty weapon, Agni shall pierce with his hurled (arrow)! [120]

When it comes to cursebreaking, there are clear advantages in knowing the curser and/or knowing the nature of the original curse. If you know the curse-caster, for example, you might include a bit of the person's hair or saliva in your countercharm. Likewise, if you're aware that the spell was put into a conjure bag and hidden somewhere in your house, you'll have a good idea of where to find the object and if you locate it, you can simply destroy it. Knowing something about the curse and its caster will definitely make things easier for the witch trying to break the spell, but such information is not an absolute necessity. In the principle of covering all bases, we find a crafty way magicians have worked around the challenge of a lack of information about the curse to be broken.

---

120   Maurice Bloomfield, *Hymns of the Atharva-Veda: Sacred Books of the East, Vol. 42* (Oxford, UK: Oxford University Press, 1897), V, 31, "Charm to Repel Sorceries or Spells," accessed March 28, 2012, http://www .sacred-texts.com/hin/sbe42/av089.htm.

In the above example from the *Atharvaveda*, a string of possibilities as to the nature of the curse are exhausted, from "The spell which they have placed down for thee in the well" to "that which they have put for thee into human bones." Several general descriptions of the identity of the curser are also included as a means to cover all bases when the specific identity of the curser is not known: "He that has undertaken it," "Him that fashions spells, practises magic, digs after roots, sends out curses." The phrase "By an unbeaten path he has brought it hither, by a (beaten) path we drive it out from here" is another means of identification—place of origin is an effective way to define the identity of the target of a spell, and even though the place named here is a vague "unbeaten path," it's named, nonetheless, and sufficient to make a positive identification of curse and curser alike. In this way, the likelihood of happening upon the identity of the curser and the nature of the original curse are greatly increased, giving the countercharm a much better chance for success. We see also in this example the reflection principle again at work, in the words "that do I hurl back again." Do you recognize any other methods of cursebreaking in this formula?

The Malay of southeast Asia also made use of the covering all the bases principle, as illustrated in this excerpt from a shaman's incantation intended to oust the demon of disease from a patient:

Where is this genie lodging and taking shelter?
Where is he lodging and crouching?
Genie! if thou art in the feet of this patient,
Know that these feet are moved by Allah and His Prophet;
If thou art in the belly of this patient,
His belly is God's sea, the sea, too, of Muhammad.
If thou art in his hands,
His hands pay homage to God and His Prophet.
If thou art in his liver, It is the secret place of God
and His Prophet!
If thou art in his heart,

His heart is Abu Bakar's palace.
If thou art in his lungs,
His lungs are 'Omar's palace.
If thou art in his spleen,
His spleen is 'Usman's palace.
If thou art in his gall-bladder,
His gall-bladder is 'Ali's palace. [121]

In this example, we find that every possibility for where the evil spirit of the illness might be currently lodging is enumerated, from the heart, to the lungs, to the belly of the inflicted. By accounting for as many possibilities as can be imagined, there is a greater chance that the baneful energy to be counteracted can be positively identified, located, and controlled.

There's another little trick being played in this charm that's also worthy of note. By dedicating the various body parts of the victim to divinities such as 'Ali, 'Usman, 'Omar, and God, the practitioner is hoping to entice these more powerful beings to intervene—yet another example of overpowering as a means of cursebreaking, and yet another instance of multi-layered magick being applied to produce the best chance of success.

Common Threads and New Perspectives

From overpowering to reflecting to destroying an object of magick, we've explored throughout this chapter many methods for breaking curses and otherwise counteracting unwelcome spells. We've learned that body-derived ingredients can provide a potent medium through which to break a curse, and we've also seen how curses and spells can be sent back to their origin through application of the reflection principle. We know also that curses and spells can be overpowered, rendered null and void by magickal energies

---

121   R. O. Winstedt, *Shaman, Saiva, and Sufi: A Study of the Evolution of Malay Magic.* Glasgow, UK: The University Press, 1925, chapter IV, "The Malay Charm." Accessed March 9, 2012. http://www.sacred-texts.com /sha/sss/sss06.htm.

that are much stronger than the original sorcery that is to be undone. So too can simply making amends and restitution to the offended party provide closure to a spell and liberation from a curse, just as destroying an object housing the magick provides quick end to the charm and instant relief. You understand the advantage of covering all the bases with your counter-charms and cursebreaking formulas, and you know a variety of ways to go about your magick. Even though actual curses are rather rare these days, cursebreaking methods can be adapted to a variety of magickal workings, making it beneficial and worthwhile to master such techniques.

Cursebreaking and Countercharms in Practice

We'll take a look at some ideas for applying cursebreaking and other forms of countermagick in your own practice, but before we do, it's important to emphasize how imperative it is to be objective in determining whether or not a curse is indeed in effect. Here are a few points to consider if you or a loved one suspects they've fallen victim to a curse.

Is It a Curse, or Just a Bad Day?

Let's admit it outright: we're all tempted to make excuses. We'd rather not take the blame for our own failures. We don't want to face the fact that the world does not always work in our favor, bending to our every need and want. In result, when we hit a stretch of misfortune that could be termed "bad luck," it's all too easy to blame it on the ex, blame it on the "fren-emy." For us magickal types especially, the awareness of the fact that being cursed by a peer is an unlikely yet very real threat is bound to make us a wee bit paranoid at times. Of course, it's not very nice to do counterac-tive magick on the innocent, so it's imperative to do your best to make sure you are indeed cursed before taking such measures. Here's a checklist to help you evaluate whether or not unsavory magickal actions have been performed against you. If few of these ring true, you're most likely just hav-ing a hard time of it lately and your misfortune will soon pass as long as you're not doing anything to self-sabotage your own success. If many of these descriptions sound like what you're going through, it might be a good time to do some defensive, cursebreaking magick to break free from what ails you; just be absolutely certain before you act, as karmic consequences may result when performing defensive magick on the innocent.

Curse Victim Diagnostic Checklist

If you're experiencing uncomfortable physical or emotional symptoms, the first thing to do is to see a qualified medical practitioner or counselor for a thorough physical checkup and/or mental evaluation. If you check out fine and yet something is still definitely amiss, get a second opinion. Remember that curses can cause real physical effects and real spiritual effects alike, so in addition to taking the most important step of seeking treatment at the mundane level, do what you can also in the cursebreaking arena to help promote your spiritual healing if you decide that you're indeed a victim of bad magick. Pay attention to your intuition and don't discount any of the following; these symptoms could be warning signs that you're under the influence of a curse:

- Have you felt unreasonably tired or weak lately? At the end of a long day, it makes sense to feel tired, but if you find yourself feeling energetic one minute and thoroughly exhausted the next minute without due cause, your tiredness might very well be a symptom of being cursed. It could be a symptom of diabetes or a host of other complaints also, so again, please do seek out a qualified professional for a full physical evaluation if you're experiencing exhaustion or any other unexplained symptoms. Make a chart to note periods in which you feel tired or weak so that you'll know the extent of the problem and can share this with your doctor. Keeping track of when and how often symptoms occur will also give you a better idea of what you're facing in terms of curse strength. Also, eat well and get plenty of rest; you'll want to rule out any obvious causes before jumping to conclusions that your tiredness is the result of a curse.

- Do you have any strong enemies who practice magick? If you're a really nice person who doesn't make many enemies, chances are, you haven't been cursed. If, on the other hand, you recently stole the High Priestess's lover away from her, you might want to take a look over your shoulder! By and large, most modern magickal practitioners do not engage in cursing magick, but some do, and that "some" can do a whole lot of damage if crossed and provoked. If you've been involved in recent quarrels, long-standing feuds, or standoffish confrontations involving people who are well-versed in the magickal arts and you find yourself suspecting you've been cursed, it's definitely worth taking a closer look at your symptoms.

- Are you having trouble making even the simplest decisions? If you're usually decisive but have lately found it difficult to make your own choices, your indecisiveness might be a curse symptom. Are you making decisions you typically wouldn't accept, choices that go against your central nature or choices that conflict with your immediate wants and needs? Sure, we sometimes have to make the tough decisions, but if you're punishing yourself with bad choices for no good reason, it's worth examining the potential causes, including the possibility of having fallen victim to a curse.

- Are you experiencing any strange or painful body sensations? Again, the first thing to do when you're experiencing physical symptoms that concern you is to see a doctor for a full evaluation to see if part of what ails you might be fixed with good old-fashioned medicine. That said, there are certain categories of discomfort that, barring obvious causes and medical explanations, are not unlikely symptoms of curse affliction. These include feelings of compression or restriction around specific body parts or affecting the body as a whole, sharp pains or very localized aches that might be constant or occur at regular or irregular intervals, extreme but brief dizziness, feeling sensations of being poked or pinched, skin that feels like it's crawling, uncomfortable prickly sensations, and shallow breathing. Any of these symptoms could be signs of a serious medical condition that may or may not have been caused by a curse; if you're experiencing any of these feelings, check it out both physically and metaphysically!

• Have you had an unexplained, severe, and unpleasant shift in mood or personality lately? Are you most often happy, but lately find yourself sinking lower and lower into a pit of depression and despair? Do you feel calm one minute, and extremely anxious the next? Do you get the feeling you're just not acting like yourself lately? Are your friends and family worried about you? If so, consult with a mental health provider or medical doctor right away for immediate help and guidance. These symptoms can be caused by a variety of conditions, and are also commonly experienced by curse victims. You might also consider doing some cursebreaking magick to help you regain your balance.

• Are you having very unusual and unlikely dreams, or do you feel exhausted when you wake up? Have you been dreaming about places and situations that have nothing at all to do with your real-life or typical dream-life experiences? Do you wake up feeling like you've run through the gauntlet, just as tired as if you hadn't slept at all? It could be just a strange dream and a night of restless sleep, but if this is happening frequently and has an uncomfortable, confused, and violated feeling associated with it, there's a possibility that you could be under the nocturnal influence of a curse that's tapping into your energies while you sleep. Try to remember the images and faces you see in such dreams—you might get a clue about the curser or their intentions.

Is It All in Your Head?

Still not sure whether or not you've been cursed? Take an objective look at the following list; if any of these leading questions ring true, it's possible that you're not the victim of a curse, but rather the victim of your own self! Are your self-sabotaging behaviors making you your own worst enemy? Ask yourself honestly and candidly:

- Do I consistently make poor decisions that I know are not in my best interest?

- Do I have any addictions that interfere with my overall success or day-to-day functioning?

- Am I neglecting any major health issues (physical or mental) that could be causing problems?

- Do I make plans, but fail to take action?

- If my ambitions were fulfilled, would it lead to a situation I wouldn't actually like?

- Do I tend to blame my own failures on outside forces and influences?

- Am I paranoid, likely to think people are against me even when there is no actual evidence to indicate it?

- Do I set only mediocre goals and fail to go after what I really want?

If you do find yourself the victim of your own curse, strive to stop sabotaging yourself! I like to call it "being your own mama"—taking care of yourself and loving yourself just as you would love your own child or cherished pet. You can also try applying some of the countermagick techniques discussed in this chapter to undo your own undoing—with the best intentions and the best techniques on your side, liberation from needless self-inflicted suffering is definitely possible!

Hopefully, you'll never have to face a magickal attack from yourself *or* from an enemy, but if you do, at least you have a few tools in your arsenal now to help see you through. Let's take a look at a couple of hypothetical modern-day examples to see how you might combine the techniques we've learned in this chapter into your own multi-layered magick strong enough to undo any spell, powerful enough to break any curse.

Cursebreaking Formula

If you're aiming to break a curse, first ask yourself what may have occurred to set the curse in motion in the first place. Did you break an oath or a pact? Did you offend a sacred place, or disturb a sacred object or powerful spirit? Did you do an injury or injustice to someone? Was the curse prompted by jealousy, justice, or revenge? If you suspect you may be even a wee bit guilty in triggering or inviting the curse that ails you, start by doing whatever you can to make amends and make it right. Do you owe anyone a favor, explanation, or apology? Can you do something special to honor the offended person, place, or spirit and win back favor? Take care of apologies and restitution first; even if further cursebreaking procedures are called for, you at least won't be hindered by lingering guilt that could otherwise hold you back and inhibit the efficacy of your magick.

If further action is indeed required, the next step is to discern as much as you can about the curse you are trying to break. Consider likely materials, methods, and deities that may have been employed in casting the original spell. Begin by taking an inventory of what you know or suspect about the curse and the curser. Consider what you know about the typical spell methods the curser employs, and the magickal and spiritual beliefs to which they adhere. You can use this information to piece together a clearer, more complete picture of the particular curse you're attempting to break. For example, if you suspect you've been cursed by an ex-lover who is a dedicant to the path of Voudon, you know there's a possibility that a powder, poppet, or gris-gris bag was employed. Likewise, if your suspected enemy frequently brags about their prowess in binding magick, you have a clear indication of the style of curse the person may have performed.

Next, evaluate the likelihood of potential cursing methods based on the proximity of the curser to the victim and on their level of trust and interaction. If the curser lives in Florida and the cursed in New York, for example, a cursing powder that administers its evils through direct contact is not likely to be the culprit. Similarly, if the suspected curser happens to be the victim's own hairdresser, the possibility of the curse including a piece of the victim's hair as a key ingredient might be worth considering.

Attempt to discern some of the more likely characteristics of the curse or other spell you're hoping to break, then choose one or more cursebreaking techniques to incorporate into your countermagick. If you don't have any information about the curse or its caster and you weren't able to intuit any best guesses, that's okay—just be sure to apply the principle of covering all the bases, and include a broad and inclusive range of possibilities whenever your countercharm design makes reference to the original spell. For example, if you can't say for sure whether you are breaking a curse cast into a doll, or a curse cast into a conjure bag, or a curse cast into something else entirely, use sweeping descriptions such as "I break the curse that was put into any medium," "I break the curse that was cast in the daytime," or "I break the curse that was cast in the nighttime." By using broad, generalized descriptions of the original spell or curse that are bound to cover all the bases in identifying whatever it is that ails you, you have a way to give your countermagick a boost. Just as identifying a curse victim by name adds power and direction to a malicious spell, so too can calling out a curse with apt description work to hinder and undo the magick.

Identifying the magick you wish to break is just one aspect of strategy. You'll also need to apply reflection, overpowering, or other cursebreaking techniques in order to undo the original charm. Remember that it might be wise to try making amends as a first line of cursebreaking magick. If making amends fails to break the spell, or is not appropriate for the situation, choose the method or methods that most appeal to you.

Now, if you are able to intuit a bit about the curse or spell you're breaking, you'll have a point of guidance in selecting your best techniques of
countermagick. For instance, if you have good reason to suspect that a curse
or undesired spell is housed within an object, and you also have a good idea
of where to find that object, then move along your countermagick efforts
with a search-and-destroy mission to seek out and smash the haunted
item. Likewise, if you feel you know who it was that cast a particular curse
you're hoping to thwart, and you have safe access to this person, you might
consider incorporating body-derived ingredients in your cursebreaking formula—it's fairly easy to find a loose hair or two on a person's unattended
jacket or coat, or even a bit of lipstick smeared on the rim of a cup. You
might burn, heat, boil, or bury such artifacts in order to destroy the curse
through sympathetic action. Remember too that ingredients derived from
the body of the curse victim can also be used to affect a healing; you might
cleanse the afflicted person in running water, or place their fingernail clippings in a dish of purifying salt and sage.

If reflection is the route you want to take to cure your curse problem,
use your words, intentions, and actions to create a reflective, reversing quality surrounding the person or place to be protected. If you're aware of any
elements of the original curse or spell you are hoping to thwart, incorporate backward, reversed, twisted versions of these same procedures, incantations, etc. For example, if you suspect the curse or spell was cast with
a candle, you might light a candle and think of it as the magick you are
attempting to break. You might extinguish the flame, then proceed to break
the candle up in to bits as you chant:

The curses into candle cast, I smash you up, away and fast! Into
darkness, magick plunged, the spell extinguished, it's undone.

If you're using this technique to undo a spell of your own making,
just change the word "curses" in this chant to "magick" or "patterns."

Whether or not you know much about the original curse, you
might incorporate reflective language in your countercharm, pronouncing

commandments such as "I send this curse back to where it came from; I reflect it back." Similarly, you might also employ reflective actions. For example, you might empower a stone to symbolize the curse you want to break, then fling this stone far away as you command the curse to go flying back to its caster. You might also use bizarre movements or words to cast your reflective countermagick—recall how the Pennsylvania Dutch turned their clothes inside out to repel gossip, and let your imagination lead the way.

If you're having trouble deciding on a method of cursebreaking, or simply feel uncomfortable taking a starring role in the procedure, consider using overpowering as your primary technique. With overpowering, you can leave the cursebreaking up to the gods and goddesses. By relying on the efficacy of prayers and pleas to a more powerful divine to overpower and overcome the infraction on one's behalf, the witch is effectively taking his or herself out of the equation, passing along the curse and the responsibility for breaking it over to the deities. Of course, many of us witches enjoy having a heavier hand in our own magick, and prefer to do the overpowering on the strength of our own magickal merit. Many witches are able to draw the power necessary to break a curse from within their own person, and prefer not to trouble the gods with requests for intervention unless it's a challenge we just can't deal with alone. Other witches find working with the deities more often can deepen one's sense of spiritual connection, and prefer to ask for guidance and help from the gods as frequently as is feasible. Whether the power is coming from you, the deities, a combination of energy from you and the deities, or another source entirely, if the energy source you are drawing on is stronger, brighter, more aggressive, and more tenacious than the energy of the original curse, it will win out every time as it outshines and overpowers the vibrational pattern of the weaker magick.

Once you've performed whatever cursebreaking actions you're going to do, strive to put the matter out of your mind. Take common sense precautions to keep yourself safe if you suspect you have an enemy out there in the world, but don't let this knowledge rule your mental or emotional state. Remain aware, alert, and confident. You might also benefit by shifting your focus to spiritual pursuits and peaceful practices such as meditation, chanting, gardening, sacred movement, magickal art, or yoga. These activities can help realign and purify your energies, giving your countermagick a better chance for success.

Magick to Counter Your Own Charms

Cursebreaking magick isn't only good for breaking curses; many of the same techniques used in cursebreaking formulas can be effectively adapted and applied to undo more positive magick of your own making. Sometimes the spells we've cast become undesirable as our needs, wants, and circumstances change. When this happens, it's nice to have a way to recall that magick before it has a chance to have further unwanted effect.

Undoing your own spellwork should be relatively easy now that you're familiar with a few methods of cursebreaking. The technique you'll use depends largely on the original design of the spell you're aiming to break, though reflection or magickal object destruction will likely prove your best bets.

If you've crafted an object in the course of the original spellcasting, simply destroying the object will neutralize the unwanted magick. For this reason, you might find it handy to include such an object in your future spell designs so you'll have a built-in way to undo the magick should it become undesirable. If there was no physical object involved in the original spellcasting, try using reflection to reverse and confuse the original magick. Consider the original actions, words, and ingredients used in the spell, then refer to these elements to recall the spell back to an earlier, malleable state. Then use reflective or bizarre language and actions to create a reflective energy surrounding the earlier magick. For instance, if in the course of the original spellcasting, you danced in a clockwise spiral and chanted "so mote it be," you might apply the reflection principle by dancing instead in a counterclockwise direction, envisioning the original magick unraveling as you chant "so won't it be!"

Remember, magickal energy, once sent, has to go *somewhere*. When undoing your own spells, try directing any lingering energies from the original spell into a brand-new bit of magick.

Points to Ponder

- Is there an ethical difference between offensive cursing magick and defensive cursebreaking magick? What is this difference exactly? Is there a line that shouldn't be crossed in terms of how far to take an act of countermagick, and if so, where is it?

- In what situations might a countercharm or countercurse be called for?

- Is a reflection spell made more powerful when its design incorporates precise knowledge about the original magick to be reversed? Can sheer intention and simple words expressing a desire for reflection be just as effective? Why or why not?

- Which method of cursebreaking magick would be best to use in a situation when time is of the essence? Which method would be best if a guarantee of success on the first try was of the utmost importance?

- Would you be willing to use cursing, countercursing, or cursebreaking magick to help thwart a murderer, rapist, or other serious threat to society? Would you be willing to use such magick to combat a global ill such as violence or hunger? Why or why not?

- What are some additional methods of cursebreaking and countermagick not discussed in this chapter?

- Can you think of any creative or non-traditional ways that techniques of cursebreaking might be applied in your own magickal practice?

NINE

Masks, Mimicry, and Magick

Since ancient times, people from many lands and many cultures have used masks, costumes, and mimicry to commune with the divine and achieve their magickal aims. From mimetic movements, dancing, and drama, to special clothing chosen for its symbolism or magickal effect, masquerade and magick go hand in hand. In the magickal adornment of our bodies, through our theatrical actions, we become more than just our everyday selves, and we're able to more readily achieve a mindset conducive to magick.

Magickal Masks and Mimicry Around the World

Erna Fergusson illustrates this rather powerful effect of masquerade blended with magick in her eloquent and visually rich description of the transformation undergone by the Hopi in preparation for an important ritual which took place as part of the *Powanu*, or Bean-Planting Ceremony, a festival held each February to help prepare the land for the crops that would soon be planted:

Lazily they rose from where they sat and, without the slightest
embarrassment, removed their shirts, trousers, and shoes, neatly
folding their things and laying them in corners. That left their
smooth brown bodies exposed, the demands of propriety being
satisfied by those modest curtains, front and back, which are
the gee-string. Each man then painted his own body, making
one leg, one arm, and one half the torso red, and the other one
white... Then each man gave a helping hand to others, painting
the backs like the fronts... Each man loosened his own hair, and
with a grass brush he curried and shook it until it lay in a shining
black mane to his waist behind and fluffed out in bobbed puffs over
his cheeks. Then he tied three of his flowers to his crown, making
a chaplet of the big gay blossoms, most effective against shining
black hair. Somewhere in this process white kirtles and sashes were
adjusted, turtle-shell rattles, strings of shell and turquoise, and
silver-studded baldrics were put on; and those ordinary young
men in faded overalls and dirty shirts were suddenly brilliant and
beautiful figures, studies in all the possible shades of red and gold
and ivory-white. [122]

The transformation from "young men in faded overalls and dirty shirts"
into impressive figures ready to play their role in the sacred dance illuminates the value and purpose of magickally meaningful attire. By dressing
the part, we're able to transcend our everyday roles. These visually striking
costumes surely added to the mystical atmosphere and magickal effect of
the ritual dance at hand. Fergusson writes:

Then... they moved into two facing lines, shifted, stamped,
rattled their gourds, and swirled into the dance. It was thrilling

---

122   Erna Fergusson, *Dancing Gods: Indian Ceremonials of New Mexico and
Arizona* (New York: Alfred A. Knopf, 1931), 131, accessed March 23,
2013, http://www.sacred-texts.com/nam/sw/dg/dg07.htm.

how quickly that hot underground room was transformed into a
chamber of mystery as those gay creatures stepped and turned and
swayed with graceful precision. Shining brown skin slipped over
muscles which were hard but never strained, hands and feet moved
rhythmically, voices chanted one of those compelling songs... Then
it seemed that there was real force in that underground prayer, a
real relationship with all the glory of the starry night outside. [123]

The build-up and play of energy, the power raised, the connection forged with "all the glory of the starry night outside"—the power of the ritual comes through loud and clear in Fergusson's description. To the Hopi as with many other mystically minded people around the world, engaging in ritual dance and donning magickal costumes helps create a very moving and meaningful experience that can be readily shared and conveyed.

The masquerade of the Powanu ceremony didn't end with the costumes and the dances. Another important part of the festival was the ceremonial planting of miniature crops of beans within the home. Small buckets or boxes were filled with dirt, bean seeds were sown, and fires were lit to help speed along germination.[124] These mini-crops mimicked the full-size crops to come, and by engaging in the masquerade of tending to them, caring for them, raising tons of magickal energy around them, the Hopi prepared the earth for farming and were thus able to help ensure a successful harvest.

The Powanu ceremony was just one of the many sacred ceremonies of the Hopi in which masquerade and mimetic movement played a role. In addition to utilizing a plethora of different dances for just as many different purposes, the Hopi also used a variety of ritual garb in their ceremonies,

---

123   Erna Fergusson, *Dancing Gods: Indian Ceremonials of New Mexico and Arizona* (New York: Alfred A. Knopf, 1931), 131–132, accessed March 23, 2013, http://www.sacred-texts.com/nam/sw/dg/dg07.htm.

124   Elisabeth Melitta Cutright-Smith, "Modeling Ancestral Hopi Agricultural Landscapes," Thesis, Dept. of Anthropology, University of Arizona (Ann Arbor, MI: ProQuest Information and Learning Company, 2007), 84.

each costume designed to complement each specific ritual, each mystical or magickal act. Special costumes consisted of jewelry, kirtles, sashes and more, often supplemented with brightly colored body paint. Colorful masks were also frequently employed. Typically designed with a ruff around the neck made of spruce, feathers, or fur, the masks concealed the entire head. The faces were painted to represent animals, monsters, birds, gods, men, or "mixed" creatures consisting of a combination of these elements. While certain masks and costumes were used year after year, others changed depending upon sudden whim or present need.[125] Masquerade as a magickal art is both fluid *and* long-standing, able to harness the immense power of tradition as well as adapt and slip seamlessly into the pressing drama of the moment.

The Iroquois also used mimetic movements and masks for a variety of magickal purposes. In *The Code of Handsome Lake, the Seneca Prophet,* by Arthur C. Parker, the following description of the I´dos, an Iroquois charm society dedicated to the welfare of animals sacred to the tribe, is related:

> *The I'dos*[126] *Company is a band of "medicine" people whose object is to preserve and perform the rites thought necessary to keep the continued good will of the "medicine" animals…*
>
> *The head singers of the I'dos are two men who chant the dance song. This chant relates the marvels that the medicine man is able to perform, and as they sing he proceeds to do as the song directs. He lifts a red-hot stone from the lodge fire and tosses it*

---

125   Erna Fergusson, *Dancing Gods: Indian Ceremonials of New Mexico and Arizona* (New York: Alfred A. Knopf, 1931), 122, accessed March 23, 2013, http://www.sacred-texts.com/nam/sw/dg/dg06.htm.

126   "I?'dos" was rendered as " I´dos" in the original text; here, the question mark denotes a full glottal stop between syllables, with stress on the first syllable. See Arthur C. Parker, *The Code of Handsome Lake, the Seneca Prophet* (Albany, NY: University of the State of New York, 1913), 129, "Key to Phonetic System," http://www.sacred-texts.com/nam/iro/parker/cohl166.htm.

like a ball in his naked hands; he demonstrates that he can see through a carved wooden mask having no eyeholes, by finding various things about the lodge; he causes a doll to appear as a living being, and mystifies the company in other ways. [127]

Here, we find that the play-act helps to build up the perceived mystique and power of the medicine man and likely does much to draw in the interest of the other ritual participants. The imitative gestures that follow the song, the trick with the red-hot stone, the creepy mask without eyeholes—all work in unison to create an atmosphere of magick and sacred mystery.

Parker also describes some of the mimetic actions, songs, and symbolic costumes of the Iroquois Eagle Society, a group dedicated to the Dew Eagle, "reviver of wilting things." The society performed healing ceremonies that were said to have a restorative effect upon the elderly and afflicted. Parker writes:

Special costumes are worn in the ceremonies. In the dance the members divide and stand opposite each other according to phratry, the animals opposite the birds. The dancers assume a squatting posture and imitate the motions of birds. The physical exertion is intense and requires constant interruption. The dancers and singers continue to dance and sing until completely exhausted, unless someone strikes the signal pole and makes a speech … After his speech, the speaker, who may be any member, presents the dancers for whom he speaks with a gift of money, tobacco, or bread: but the old custom was to give only such things as birds liked for food. [128]

127   Arthur C. Parker, *The Code of Handsome Lake, the Seneca Prophet* (Albany, NY: University of the State of New York, 1913), 122–123, "Society of Mystic Animals," accessed March 23, 2013, http://www.sacred-texts.com/nam/iro/parker/cohl154.htm.

128   *Ibid.,* 124–125.

The costumed dancers mimic the motion of birds, representing the healing Dew Eagle to which their clan is dedicated. By becoming the human
embodiment of the Dew Eagle, a connection is forged between the dancers
and the divine. The dancers dress like the Dew Eagle, move like the Dew
Eagle, and receive offerings like the Dew Eagle—therefore, they're able to
heal like the Dew Eagle. The costumes, the dance, the masquerade combine
in a play that allows for the transmission of healing energies, from the gods,
to the "birds," to the sick.

In China also, animal costumes were employed in ritual contexts. Shamans wore animal masks, skins, and furs, and even adopted animal postures and movements during certain rituals. One annual festival called the
Nuo incorporated animal disguises in exorcism rites intended to drive away
drought, demons, and other evils. In his 2002 work *The Animal and the
Daemon in Early China*, Roel Sterckx highlights the use of costume during
the Nuo; while the shaman brandished a lance and battled with invisible
evils, masked animal attendants scared away danger with their ferocious
expressions and movements:

> *The shaman was accompanied by twelve attendants disguised as
> spirit beasts wearing fur, feathers, and horns. A spell was chanted
> to urge these costumed actors to devour a host of evils ... Various
> other officials put on wooden animal masks to participate in
> the exorcisms. The identification with animal powers enacted
> by disguising the face with an animal mask or by wearing its
> skin reinforced the officiant's power to deter malign influences
> through the medium of a monstrous facial expression.* [129]

Animal-themed ritual masks were also employed by Yupik shamans
in Alaska. Some masks represented the spirits residing over various game

---

[129]   Roel Sterckx, *The Animal and the Daemon in Early China* (Albany, NY:
State University of New York Press, 2002), 188.

animals, important to the survival of the people. One such mask was encircled with a hoop of animal images, while another included a raven holding other animals captive in its beak and feet. The shamans used the masks to help them invoke the spirits in charge of each game animal and thus ascertain whether or not there would be enough animals available to sustain the people.[130] In a contribution included in the 2004 compilation, *Shamanism: An Encyclopedia of World Beliefs, Practices, and Culture, Volume I*, Jean-Loup Rousselot describes the extent to which the shamans gave themselves over to the spirits:

> *When the shaman wore this mask, he acted as if he were the spirit itself, deciding whether to give the game to the people. The shaman was no longer asking for game, but instead incorporated the spirit that was master of the game. The spirit announced his decision, speaking through the mouth of the shaman.*[131]

In South America, The Incas also used special costumes for mystical purposes. At the *Yahuayra* festivals, held each July in order to help ensure the successful growth of the food supply, clothing was an important aspect of celebration. Long red shirts which stretched all the way down to the feet were worn as songs and chants for prosperity were performed.[132] Red was a symbol of power, authority, and creation to the Incas, and the use of red

130   Jean-Loup Rousselot, "Yupik and Inupiaq Masks (Alaska)," in *Shamanism: An Encyclopedia of World Beliefs, Practices, and Culture, Volume I*, edited by Mariko Namba Walter, Eva Jane Neumann Fridman (Santa Barbara: ABC-CLIO Inc., 2004), 360–361.

131   *Ibid.*, 361.

132   Christoval De Molina, "The Fables and Rites of the Yncas," in *Narratives of the Rites and Laws of the Yncas*, edited and translated by Clements R. Markham (London: Hakluyt Society, 1873), "July," accessed March 23, 2013, http://www.sacred-texts.com/nam/inca/rly/rly1.htm.

ritual garments was meant to attract the attention and notice of the gods.[133] By adding powerful earth energy to the agricultural ritual at hand, the potency of the chanted prayers could be increased.

In an essay written in 1873, Christoval De Molina recounts the Incan *Situa* festival, held each August in hopes of warding off sickness:

> *All things having been arranged, the High Priest addressed the assembly, and said that the ceremonies of the Situa should be performed, that the Creator might drive all the diseases and evils from the land. A great number of armed men, accoutred for war, with their lances, then came to the square in front of the temple… Then the people, who were armed as if for war, went to the square of Cuzco, crying out: "O sicknesses, disasters, misfortunes, and dangers, go forth from the land." In the middle of the square, where stood the urn of gold which was like a fountain, that was used at the sacrifice of chicha, four hundred men of war assembled. One hundred faced towards Colla-suyu, which is the direction of the Sun-rising. One hundred faced to the westward, which is the direction of Chinchasuyu. Another hundred looked towards Antisuyu, which is the north, and the last hundred turned towards the south. They had with them all the arms that are used in their wars… they cried out and said: "Go forth all evils."* [134]

The men then fly out in every direction, shouting away all evils as they make a mock charge on the invisible dangers they hope to divert. By acting out the masquerade of waging war on illness, disaster, and other misfortunes, the Inca sent a clear message to their deity, expressing their united intention with creativity as well as passion and flair. The impressive warrior garb

---

133   Elena Phipps, *Cochineal Red: The Art History of a Color* (New York: Metropolitan Museum of Art, 2010), 24.

134   De Molina, *op. cit.*, "August."

coupled with the sheer number of participants involved in this ritual must have been quite awe-inspiring to witness, and magickally very powerful.

The Olmec also enjoyed a little magickal masquerade. In Olmec culture, an early civilization centered in south central Mexico, masks symbolizing gods, humans, and archetypes were employed for a variety of purposes. While many masks were made of clay, others were crafted from more precious materials such as jade and serpentine. Wearing the mask of a god was believed to confer divine power to the wearer, while a portrait mask representing the face of an ancestor might be worn to help a person connect with and honor the dead. Sometimes, masks were included on statuary, figurines, and other artifacts depicting the gods, used to emphasize the alternative identities and attributes of the deities. Masks were even used in death in Olmec society, placed on the face of the corpse to forever mimic their living features and thus magickally stave off decay. [135]

The Olmec crafted masks in a variety of sizes, from face size to oversize to tiny. Olmec mini-masks, called maskettes, typically measured about 3 inches in diameter and bore a drilled hole on each side so that it could be attached to an object or suspended from a cord. These small masks may have been used as pendants, as adornments for headdresses, or as decoration for miniature idols. [136]

Special costumes were worn for many Olmec rites and ceremonies throughout the year, and masks were an important aspect of the sacred garb. Often, ceremonial masks blended characteristics of human, god, and beast. The Olmec mask used to depict the "were-jaguar" rain god, for example, typically had a large protruding upper lip like a jaguar, yet

---

135   Peter David Joralemon, "The Olmec," in *The Face of Ancient America: The Wally and Brenda Zollman Collection of Precolumbian Art,* edited by Lee A. Parsons, John B. Carlson, and Peter David Joralemon (Indianapolis, IN: Indianapolis Museum of Art, 1988), 36.

136   *Ibid.,* 38.

human-like almond-shaped eye holes and a trapezoidal-shaped mouth hole typically found on masks portraying humans. [137]

Olmec shamans wore such masks to activate their inner connection to the spirit animal or deity therein represented, the costume helping along the ritual transformation from human to divine. Individual shaman had their own *naualli*, or spirit animal companion, with which they were associated. Through the use of masks, figurines, and other aids such as hallucinogens, drumming, meditation, and dance, the shamans entered a trance state in which they could travel between planes of reality. [138]

Ceremonial masks are still used in modern Mexico, incorporated into dramatic dances performed to mark religious days and historical events. Just as in ancient times, in some places the masks are believed to actually embody the spirit of the animal or entity represented, thus keeping the wearer safe and protected during ritual. Some masks are recycled: they're given a fresh coat of paint and reused year after year, while other masks are destroyed straightaway after the ceremony. [139]

During modern Day of the Dead festivities, participants carry on the traditional practice of wearing masks or face paint to resemble the many aspects of death. These costumes vary widely, though the death theme is featured throughout. Some masks show a more comical aspect of death, depicting grinning skeletons, while other corpse-like masks appear more sinister and grotesque, complete with rotting teeth or other ugly features.[140] By dressing as the dead, people show respect for ancestors, facilitate communication with the spirit world, and learn to accept the natural process of

---

137   Peter David Joralemon, *op. cit.*, 36.

138   Christopher A. Pool, *Olmec Archaeology and Early Mesoamerica* (Cambridge, UK: Cambridge University Press, 2007), 173–174.

139   Marion Oettinger, Jr., *Folk Treasure of Mexico: The Nelson A. Rockefeller Collection* (Houston, TX: Arte Publico Press, 2012), 35.

140   Deborah Bell, *Mask Makers and their Craft: An Illustrated Worldwide Study* (Jefferson, MO: McFarland and Co., 2010), 98–99.

living and dying. Through the use of costume, a bridge is forged between the living and the dead, between the undesired and the unavoidable. Death is inevitable, and in Mexico, play-acting the part in advance has been a long-standing way to cope with and transcend the fear of dying that plagues us all.

In Switzerland as well, special costumes were employed for sacred purposes. In *Festivals of Western Europe*, a 1958 work by Dorothy Gladys Spicer, the use of masks during Carnival, or *Fastnacht*, a festival celebrated to mark an end to winter, is described:

> *Carnival is celebrated extensively throughout the country, with each town and village following its own local traditions. At Flums, near the Wallensee, for example, celebrants in wooden masks (many of which are handed down from father to son for generations) parade through the streets. It is thought that these horrible and terrifying masks, some of which symbolize abstract ideas such as war, death or disease, originally were made to dissipate the very forces they so hideously represent.*
>
> *At Einsiedeln, in Schwyz, "Carnival Runners," wearing grotesque false faces and with enormous bells attached to their backs, run through the streets continuously from Sunday to Ash Wednesday morning. The bells, which are so heavy the men have to bend their backs to support the weight, clang incessantly as the Runners course through the town. This ceremony, like the masks of Flums, also survives from ancient times when primitive people "drove out Winter" with deafening noise and fearsome faces and "rang in" their welcome to the Spring.*[141]

---

141   Dorothy Gladys Spicer, *Festivals of Western Europe* (New York: H.W. Wilson Company, 1958), Section 12, "Festivals of Switzerland," accessed March 23, 2013, http://www.sacred-texts.com/etc/fwe/fwe14.htm.

The rather scary masks employed in these ceremonies work to repel unwanted energies through mimicry. By embodying and imitating war, disease, or other frightening aspects of society, and by taking the mimicry a step further by being even more repulsive than these ills, the masks have a reflective quality that can send these unfortunate energies packing. So too does the bell ringing, running, and parading operate in mimetic fashion, symbolizing through various means and mediums the same basic notion of good triumphing over evil, vitality and strength prevailing over misfortune. We see in this example that both costumes and dramatic, mimetic action combine to produce the intended result, be it to welcome the spring or to drive off winter, war, death, or disease. The action of the celebrants with their masks and parade at Flums, the action of the Carnival Runners with their equally bizarre masks and loud raucous at Einsiedeln, represent sacred dramas of sorts, ritually enacted make-believe intended to have real magickal effects.

Fastnacht is still widely celebrated today, and large-scale masquerade still plays a major part in the festivities. According to www.myswitzerland.com, the official website of Switzerland tourism, the Fasnacht carnival held each year in Basel boasts an average 15,000 to 20,000 masked participants! [142]

In ancient Greece, such large-scale community rites and festivals were common, with costume, drama, and ritual blending into a singular magickal experience. An excerpt from Harold R. Willoughby's 1929 work *Pagan Regeneration* provides a succinct overview of known facts about an Eleusinian passion play that highlights the interactive and improvisational nature of Greek magickal drama used to mimic the gods:

The abduction of Persephone, the grief of her mother, the search for the lost daughter, and the reunion of the two goddesses—these were

---

142   Official Website of Switzerland Tourism, MySwitzerland.com, "Fastnacht in Basel (BS)," accessed March 23, 2013, http://www.myswitzerland.com/en/fasnacht-in-basel-bs.html.

*the principle scenes… Clad in gorgeous and traditional costumes
the personages of the Eleusinian passion play must have been very
impressive figures. Of scenic effect there was little or nothing… Greek
audiences, like the spectators of the Elizabethan drama, were trained
to depend upon their imaginations to supply what was lacking in stage
settings. So at Eleusis, the effectiveness of the passion play depended
much upon the cultivated imaginations of the mystae. Moreover, by
simple expedients the participation of the initiates in the action of
the drama was brought about. They were not merely spectators of a
pageant; they were participants in a ritual. The gong focused their
attention upon the first great crisis of the drama, the abduction of the
daughter. With torches they followed the mother in her frantic search
and again with the waving of torches they expressed their joy at the
return of her daughter. Thus, by participation in the dramatic action,
as well as by active imagination, the mystae were enabled to share
emotionally in the experiences of the great goddesses.* [143]

Willoughby's summation of the Eleusinian ritual as allowing the participants to emotionally connect with the deities could hold equally true
for many acts of mimetic magick around the globe. Through ceremonial
costumes, sacred drama and dance, through dress-up and make-believe,
we become as the gods, creating new worlds and new realities with our
magickal play.

Common Threads and New Perspectives

Throughout this chapter, we've seen how people around the world have
used masquerade and mimicry to enhance their magickal arts. Successful

---

143   Harold R. Willoughby, *Pagan Regeneration: A Study of Mystery Initiations
in the Graeco-Roman World* (Chicago: University of Chicago Press, 1929),
Chapter II, accessed March 23, 2013, http://www.sacred-texts.com/cla/pr/
pr04.htm.

magick requires us to step up from mundane reality and step out of our everyday roles; in this way, we achieve a magickal mindset that allows us to use emotionally charged thought to manifest and mold the world around us. Through the use of magickal costumes and mimetic drama, we're able to enter a ritual consciousness more readily. Masks, jewelry, and other magickally charged and attuned garb can make us feel like more than we typically are; by donning the head of a lion, we become like a lion, pushing fear from the mind as courage swells in the heart. We're not only better able mentally to work the magick at hand, but also we enjoy the benefit of having more power available with which to cast the spell. As we've seen from some of the examples in this chapter, a simple mask can have within it the power of the beasts, the power of the gods—when we work magick wearing special clothing and costume, the energy within the fashions themselves can enhance the overall effect of our rites.

Using masks and costumes can have other benefits, as well. Extraordinary clothing creates an extraordinary atmosphere and mystical ambiance just right for ritual. Further, wearing a magickal costume can help us magickally connect—with the gods, with our spirit animals, and even with the dead.

So too does the act of engaging in mimetic drama help us weave threads between ourselves and the deities, between individual magick worker and universal magickal power. By imitating what the gods do, by imitating what we wish to happen as if our play-acting will make it so, our magick has a strong foundation on which to rest. Imitative, mimetic actions are at the heart of many a magickal formula. It's simply one of the easiest, most reliable ways to create a living symbol, a message or code of sorts, that conveys to the "above" what we wish to occur "below." Magick is make-believe, and through masquerade and mimicry, the belief we need to make the world as we choose comes as naturally as child's play.

Magickal Mask-Making

If the examples in this chapter have inspired you, why not try crafting your own special costumes for magick? You might make a cloak, a robe, a headdress, or even a mask.

One easy technique for making a magickal mask is to create it out of papier-mâché formed over the front half of an inflated balloon. Begin by blowing up a balloon so that it's about the same size as your head. Next, hold a piece of flexible paper over your face, and mark the eyes, nose, and mouth areas. Use this paper as a stencil to mark out the places on the balloon where the air and vision holes will go. Cut an old newspaper into strips that are roughly one inch wide and about five or six inches long. Dip the paper one strip at a time in a shallow dish of glue or paste. Let the excess sticky stuff drip off, then delicately place the paper strip on the balloon, smoothing out any wrinkles so that it lies perfectly flat upon the surface of the balloon. Continue placing paper strips in this manner one at a time, overlapping the strips and letting the mask dry between layers. Basically, the paper and glue combine to harden into a stiff shell. Plenty of overlap, plenty of glue, and plenty of drying time between layers is essential.

Once you have a good base layer of the mask going on, the entire face area minus the eye, nose, and mouth holes covered with at least a few layers of the paper strips, think about the basic form of your mask if you haven't done so already. Will it have any appendages, such as a snout, or perhaps a pair of long, pointy ears? If so, use small pieces of cardboard, cut and folded to shape, to create the structural elements of your mask. Use duct tape or another sturdy tape to attach the cardboard directly onto the papier-mâché, then add more paper strips on top of and around these additions to strengthen the bond and even out the texture of the mask.

Once your mask is complete and you have at least ⅛ to ¼ of an inch or so layer of papier-mâché, make sure it's all dry, then pop the balloon and remove it from the mask. Add holes at the sides of your mask so that you can attach a string or elastic band.

Paint the mask any way you like, and decorate it according to its function. Magickally charged and intuitively or intentionally selected natural items such as feathers, stones, sticks, nut shells, seed hulls, leaves, and bark make fine additions to your mask.

The Story of Your Life

Another adventure in magickal mimicry you might want to try is choreographing your own ritual dance or Mystery play. Challenge yourself to come up with your own special dance or drama in honor of your essence; tell the story of your life through your movements and expressions. Tell also your future story, your goals, dreams, and intentions that you wish to weave into the fibers of your history. Consider tradition when choreographing your dance or play. What imitative motions might you include? At what points will the dance or drama build in power? Would it be helpful to wear a special costume while performing your story? How will the intention of the dance or drama be expressed, and how will the energy of that intention be released to the wider world to do your bidding? Once you've decided on some basics and have practiced a bit, note those places of rising power that can be utilized as optimal send-off points for your magickal intentions and tweak your performance to take advantage of these natural peaks. If you feel comfortable, make a video of your practice sessions for later review. In this way, you can continue to hone your mimetic dance or drama as your skills in mystical self-expression further unfold.

Points to Ponder

- Thinking back to when you played make-believe as a child, do you see any parallels between imaginative play and mimetic magick? Can you remember any childhood games that might provide inspiration for spellwork involving mimicry, imitative gestures, or costumes?

- Do you think that wearing special clothing or masks when performing a ritual has an effect on the practitioner's mental or spiritual state?

- Do you ever feel that your mood or mental state are affected by what you're wearing? If so, how might you play up this effect to your advantage?

- Consider how magicians past and present have used magickal masks to frighten away threats, enhance personal power, and connect to the deities. What other applications of magickal masks can you think of?

- How might a mask made to represent one of your most unpleasant anxieties or characteristics be employed to help you diminish or alter these limitations?

- How might a mask made to resemble and embody a deity to whom you're dedicated help you forge a connection with this god? Might you feel more empowered to work powerful magick when dressing the part of the divine?

- This chapter discussed specifically the use of masquerade and mimicry in the magickal arts. Might it be argued, however, that nearly *all* magick is mimetic? Why or why not? Can you identify any major points of difference in magick that could be classified as mimetic, or imitative, and magick that doesn't fall into this category? What are the differences?

ten

Group Magick

Since ancient times, people have practiced magick in groups. From ancient Greek Mystery schools to modern covens in America, our magickal practice builds community. We come to feel close to our covenmates; in sharing a simple ritual, a lifetime of friendship is often forged. For the solitary practitioner who has never or seldom before cast magick in a group setting, the benefits of doing so can seem a little vague or questionable. For the experienced group practitioner, the challenges of cooperative magick are just as familiar and apparent as are the potential benefits. After all, there's a fine line between healthy, functioning group and malignant, dysfunctional, might-as-well-be-a-church. While state-sponsored public rituals and magick rites have indeed traditionally offered government leaders a handy way to guide, direct, motivate, and manage their populations, working magick in groups need not be in the form of a flock of sheep following the leader. Group magick can in fact be far more liberating and rewarding than the outward structure of hierarchy, rules, and restrictions might imply.

Group magick and community-wide ritual workings indeed provide a host of real benefits to the group as well as to the individual. Even solitaries find benefit in working magick with others from time to time; in sharing our magick, we share the work, as well. It makes sense that magick worked with other witches is generally more powerful than magick cast alone—we add our own personal power to the spells we cast, and with more people involved, there's naturally more power available. More people to summon helpful and necessary energies, more people to solidify the intention, more people to code the energy, more people to magnify the power, and more people to release the spell typically equates to more effective magick with half the work as would usually be required for a solitary casting. Multiple-person spellwork also allows for specialization—with lots of friends to help, each person can focus on their own particular abilities and aptitudes, making it possible to have an expert to handle each part of the magick.

There's also the advantage of having more third eyes available to seek out hidden options and identify potential problems. When we're personally invested in our spells (as we should be), it's very easy to overlook the obvious, and having more people involved in the magick means you have some buddies on hand who can hopefully catch any mistakes before they're made. Having a magickal think tank behind you makes spellcrafting easier, as there are more minds to brainstorm ways to craft a spell that's truly a magickal masterpiece, just right for the situation at hand.

Working magick in groups is not only practical for magickal reasons; it's a practice that also appeals to and satisfies our need for socialization. Group magick provides opportunities for communication, interaction, and camaraderie. It can literally craft a community, creating a set of common goals and common worldviews that guide our everyday dealings with the people around us. In an essay included in *Handbook of the Sociology of Emotions*, Erika Summers-Effler explains the importance of group ritual in shaping our social interactions, cultures, and day-to-day lives:

> *Rituals generate group emotions that are linked to symbols,*
> *forming the basis for beliefs, thinking, morality, and culture.*
> *People use the capacity for thought, beliefs, and strategy to*
> *create emotion-generating interactions in the future.*

This cycle, interaction—emotions—symbols—interaction, forms
patterns of interaction over time. These patterns are the most
basic structural force that organizes society.[144]

Sharing ritual with others creates both a shared mentality and a shared emotional experience—in effect, a collective group consciousness. When we participate in a ritual together, we talk in the symbolic language of magick, creating new common patterns of ideas and beliefs with which to base our understanding of ourselves, our communities, and our world. Just as group magick enhances our individual understanding of society as a whole, so too are our one-on-one interactions with each other strengthened and enriched through the experience of working magick together.

If you sometimes feel a little lost or lonely in your spiritual practice, or if you ever wish you could have just a little extra power and help with a magickal working, you might want to consider giving group magick a try. Community and friendship are not wants, after all, but needs, not to mention the fact that group magick can be a very powerful and transformative process for the individuals participating. In sharing magick and ritual with others, friendships are born and strong feelings of interconnection and trust emerge. As Skott Holck, leader of a small Wiccan coven in Denver, Colorado, puts it, "A coven should be a bond like a family, but so much more. Working magick is all about improving yourself, and having a support structure around you as you grow is a great benefit. When we need something, we can turn to our coven mates and know support will be given. Also, during some vulnerable moments in Circle, it is nice to know that people who care about you are there."

This simple principle of camaraderie is as worthwhile today as it has been for centuries. Liking each other and learning from each other

---

144   Erika Summers-Effler, "Ritual Theory," in *Handbook of the Sociology of Emotions,* ed. Jan E. Stets and Jonathan H. Turner (New York: Springer Science + Business Media, 2007), 135.

are quite natural inclinations, after all, and coming together for magick and ritual is both our instinct and our heritage.

Let's now take a look at some concrete examples of group magick from around the world. By exploring the common threads that weave these different traditions together, you'll discover how to use group magick more creatively and more effectively for both your personal benefit and for the benefit of your community as a whole.

Group Magick Around the World

Spellcasters and magick weavers around the world have practiced magick in groups for many purposes, from building community to securing a good harvest to adding power to a particular magickal working. Let's take a closer look at a few of the more common motivators for group magick worldwide.

More Music for More Ears

Music is a well-known and effective medium, catalyst, and facilitator of magick. Even a one-man band can do much with the magick of music, and when we create our music with others, the possibilities become richer and the process is more rewarding. Ancient and modern magicians alike have recognized this simple truth and in result have found their way to group magick and music.

To the ancient Dionysians, music was an integral part of group ritual. One of many important magickal groups in ancient Greece, the cult of Dionysus was originally believed to have been imported from Thrace or Phrygia. However, inscriptions to a DI-WO-NO-SO-JO found on a Mycenean tablet written in Linear B, the second oldest known Greek script, indicate that the cult may have its origins in a nature religion indigenous to Greece that dates back to 1200 BCE or earlier. [145]

As the god of wine and passion, Dionysus was worshiped and celebrated widely, often with drums, singing, dancing, and the music of the

---

[145] John Paul Adams, "Dionysos," January 23, 2010, California State University, accessed March 23, 2013, http://www.csun.edu/~hcfll004/dionysos.html.

aulos, a type of double-pipe wind instrument from which the oboe got its origins. Group rites ranged from private ceremonies open only to initiates, to large public festivals, feasts, and processions involving the wider community. Dionysus was representative of wild abandon, offering followers a reason and a means to shed inhibitions and enjoy the moment. [146]

In ancient Greece, Dionysus was celebrated with many prominent community-wide rites throughout the year. Music was a big part of these ceremonies, which were often enhanced with strong visual symbolism in addition to the auditory effects. One important tradition was the phallus procession, in which representations of penises—called phalli—in varying sizes were paraded through the town in honor of Dionysus and in hopes of procuring fertility of the crops and of the people. The phalli were typically made of wood, leather, or stone, and some were small enough to be handheld. Others were much larger, and had to be rolled on a cart. In *The Sex of Men in Premodern Europe: A Cultural History*, Patricia Simons provides a description of these phallic sacred objects:

> *While many were hand-held, representations of the larger processional type tend to show it looking like a large log pulled on a cart or carried by a group of bearers…*
>
> *On many occasions, a system of ropes or strings ensured that the phallos was a puppet, rising up and down in the parade, which would have accentuated the seasonal changes of the agricultural cycle but also provided a degree of levity, in both the literal and figurative senses.* [147]

---

146   For more information on Dionysian ritual, see "Women on the Mountain: Exploring the Dionysiac Mysteries," Robert Leary, Thesis presented to Ohio University, 2010, accessed March 23, 2013, at http://etd.ohiolink.edu/send-pdf.cgi/Leary%20Robert .pdf?ouhonors1282940703.

147   Patricia Simons, *The Sex of Men in Premodern Europe: A Cultural History* (Cambridge, UK: Cambridge University Press, 2011), 53.

As the penis cart rolled through the streets, singers sung songs rife with phallic humor and adulation. Although one result of the phallic procession was certain to have been laughter and levity (Aristotle believed it to be the origin of stand-up comedy), the fake penis parade and its accompanying music held deep significance not only for the followers of Dionysus, but for the community as a whole. The phallic procession promoted fertility of both the crops and the people, and also offered protection for the entire city. Even for those community members not directly associated with Dionysus's cult, the large public festivities held in honor of this god were a sight to behold and could not be missed.

Of their private rites, little is known, though we can ascertain that Dionysus's followers used a combination of group music, intoxicants, costume, mimicry, and revelry to achieve their magickal and spiritual aims, which were focused in part on embracing the natural instinct. With wild music, dancing, and magick mingled, rituals were primal and passionate, creating a state of ecstasy in which the whole group could share. Sometimes the rituals were bloody, involving the ritualistic killing and consumption of snakes and small wild animals.[148]

The collective frenzy enjoyed by the cult of Dionysus in both their public rites and private rites not only allowed for a powerful shared experience, but also provided a very large generator of magickal energy. It's hard to imagine that a Dionysian rite in which devotees don animal skins, shed their inhibitions, and allow the sounds of the drums, the aulos, and their own voices to open the door to ecstasy, would have quite the same effect or potential if performed by a solitary practitioner with only one voice with which to sing, one drum on which to play.

The cult of the Mother of the Gods was another important mystery cult that made prominent use of music, with groups spread throughout

---

148   Barbara F. McManus, "Background and Images for the Bacchae," 1999, accessed March 23, 2013, http://www2.cnr.edu/home/bmcmanus/bacchaebg.html.

the ancient Greco-Roman world. Her origins in the older nature religions of Asia Minor and in particular Phrygia, the Mother of the Gods was imported into Rome by decree of the Senate in 204 BCE, in response to an oracle predicting that doing so would be beneficial to the state.[149]

The Roman worship of the Mother of the Gods was much more tame and controlled than was her original worship. While state-sponsored public ceremonies were held for her annually, the goddess's own foreign priests took care of the more exotic aspects of rituals held in her honor. For instance, there was an important blood-letting ceremony in which the altar of the goddess was sprinkled with the blood of her priests. These priests were Phrygians who had traveled to Rome alongside the imported goddess, and Roman citizens were prohibited from taking part in these exclusively Phrygian rituals.

Just as music played a major role in the rituals of the cult of Dionysus, so too were the musical arts important to the cult of the Mother of the Gods. Her followers got together and celebrated with singing, dancing, drums, and pipes, as well, though again, these practices were reserved exclusively for her Phrygian worshipers. The timpano drum was especially associated with this goddess of many names, and her followers also made use of castanets to achieve a powerful rhythm conducive to a trance state. The Phrygian followers of the Mother of the Gods also practiced castration, and processions were held in which the dedicated worshipers would carry a chariot-bound idol of the goddess through the streets, asking for alms from the general Roman citizenry who were forbidden from taking direct part in the procession. A good portion of the Roman citizenry was most welcome, however, to take full part in the Megalesia, a festival held in honor of the Mother of the Gods each April. Festivities included games, theatrical performances, ritual feasts, and sacrifices. To the Phrygian priests

---

149   Rodney Stark, *Discovering God: The Origins of the Great Religions and the Evolution of Belief* (New York: Harper Collins, 2007), 137–139.

and priestesses who directly participated in her worship, rites were ecstatic and had much in common with wild and raucous Dionysian rituals. [150, 151]

The Aztecs also held group rituals, and like the Dionysians and the cult of the Mother of the Gods, they too made use of music to enhance their ceremonies. Favoring ceramic flutes, drums, rasps made from human bones, rattles, whistles, and trumpet-like instruments made from conch shells, the Aztecs made music an important part of their magickal rites. In a ritual to Tezcatlipoca, the Aztec god of the nocturnal sky, ancestral memory, and time, musicians would finish their set by smashing their flutes. Numerous flutes and flute fragments have been excavated at Tenochtitlan, offering evidence of large-scale ritualistic workings involving group music. [152]

Many African tribes practiced group magick incorporating music, as well. In Uganda, for instance, certain rituals among the various tribes often included the use of drums, rattles, xylophones, and string instruments such as the *edongo*, or bowl lyre. [153]

Drama and Dance

Another practical reason for group magick is that it makes possible a great variety of ritual drama and dance. Archeology has unearthed plenty of

---

150   For more information, see Sir James George Frazer, *The Golden Bough* (1922; repr., New York: Bartleby.com, 2000), Chapter 34, "The Myth and Ritual of Attis," accessed January 9, 2012, http://www.bartleby.com/196/.

151   See also Philippe Borgeaud, *Mother of the Gods: From Cybele to the Virgin Mary,* translated by Lysa Hochroth (Baltimore, MD: The John Hopkins University Press, 2004), 62–66.

152   Michael E. Smith, "Aztecs," in *The Oxford Handbook of the Archaeology of Ritual and Religion,* edited by Timothy Insoll (New York: Oxford University Press, 2011), 562.

153   Face Music. "Traditional Instruments of the Uganda People," "Traditional Dance of the Uganda People," accessed March 23, 2013, http://www.face-music.ch/instrum/uganda_instrumen.html, http://www.face-music.ch/instrum/uganda_danceen.html.

evidence of the long history of both drama and dance, and both disciplines seem to have roots in group ritual. The Bhimbetka rock shelters in India contain rock paintings dating from c. 3300 BCE depicting communal dances and figures bearing body art that may have had symbolic meaning or purpose,[154] while Egyptian texts dating from 2800 BCE to 2400 BCE describe dramas depicting the story of Osiris and other important myths.[155] These spiritually meaningful and symbolic dances and plays would be hard to perform with one dancer, one actor alone. Our natural propensity to tell stories, to share myths, to express truths with our bodies and souls, has led people throughout the ages to embrace group dance and drama as a means of magick as well as a means of teaching and making merry. Dance and drama, like music, gives us yet more reasons to come together in numbers for our magick and rituals.

Specialization

Yet another practical advantage to working magick in groups is that it allows for specialization. By having more people available to pitch in and take care of the magickal needs of the community, it becomes possible for individuals or smaller groups within the larger group to focus on a particular area or areas of magickal expertise. In Aboriginal society, for example, various clans were responsible for magickally assuring the abundance of certain animal populations.[156] Each clan dedicated to its respective animal, within

---

154   Dr. Somnath Chakraverty, *Rock Art and Tribal Art of India*, "Bhimbetka: the Glimpses of Indian Rock-Art in a World Heritage Site," accessed March 23, 2013, http://rockartandtribalartofindia.blogspot.com/2010/07/bhimbetka-glimpses-of-indian-rock-art.html.

155   Scott R. Robinson, "Origins of Theatre," Central Washington University, accessed March 23, 2013, http://www.cwu.edu/~robinsos/ppages/resources/Theatre_History/Theahis_1.html.

156   William Howell Edwards, *An Introduction to Aboriginal Societies* (South Melbourne, AU: Social Science Press, 2004), 80.

certain clans, eating the meat of said animal was off limits.[157] This system allowed for individuals who perhaps have a deeper connection with a particular animal to use this relationship to the advantage of the community in working magick to help propagate said species.

Many indigenous cultures of the Americas also found specialization to be a benefit of group magick. The Seneca, for instance, had a large number of individual clans responsible for their own respective realms of influence. Among these were the Dawando`, a society of women dedicated to the propagation of otters and other water animals, as well as the Husk Faces, a loosely organized group of water doctors that healed by spraying or sprinkling water on the inflicted. [158]

In many modern magickal groups, we also specialize, with certain people casting the circle, or perhaps administering the wine and cakes, etc. However, we don't seem to see nearly the level of specialization that our magickal ancestors enjoyed. Perhaps in expanding our groups to larger proportions, perhaps in focusing our efforts on discovering and utilizing the unique talents of everyone involved in a magickal working, we'll come to embrace our niches and learn to excel in our personal areas of interest and mastery.

Same Old Story

Another practical reason people come together for magick and ritual is as old as the hills and as current as tomorrow: yep, that's right—for the hookup. Not to imply that the hope of winning love or at least temporary sexual gratification is the main motivator of group magick; many magick groups have no physically intimate interaction at all, and even for those who do, there are typically far greater goals at hand than the immediate pleasure that such interactions might trigger in the moment. Still, we can't deny the

---

157   Enotes.com, "Australian Aborigines," accessed March 23, 2013, http://www.enotes.com/australian-aborigines-reference/australian-aborigines.

158   Arthur C. Parker, *The Code of Handsome Lake, the Seneca Prophet.* 1913. Repr., Charleston, SC: BiblioBazaar, LLC, 2008, 171–172, 187–188.

fact that many people do indeed come to community circles and festivals and such at least in part in the hopes of meeting a long-term partner or a short-term lover. The phenomenon is nothing new.

In the days before TV and Internet arrived to pacify, entertain, and temper our human urges for real-life social interaction, community festivals, public magickal rites, and membership in magickal "clubs" such as the Greek mystery schools all served a very important function: they provided an opportunity for people to come together around a common purpose and hopefully bond a little. Ancient Celtic Beltane celebrations, for instance, brought women and men together to gather flowers and build bonfires. The atmosphere of the celebrations was festive and overtly sexual, often leading to the forging of real romantic partnerships. [159]

Present-day examples are also easy to find: take a trip to any of the major Pagan festivals in the country, and you're likely to run into at least a few individuals who seem to have their minds set on hooking their claws into someone tasty—not that that's always a bad thing! The desire for intimacy and interaction doesn't necessarily take precedence over one's magickal goals, and acknowledging our human condition of wanting each other and wanting to be wanted is an honest admission that allows us to see another layer of value in our magickal group workings.

Common Threads and New Perspectives

When we compare the magick groups of today to the magick groups of the distant past, several similarities are apparent. We still like to get together to make our magick, and our community rituals and public rites often include the use of music, dance, and drama, just as they did in the times of ancient Greece and pre-colonial Africa. Our group structures are also similar—in modern times as well as in the past, our group workings are typically guided by a leader or class of leaders, and each and every participant in the ritual

---

159   "Beltane," BBC.com, accessed March 24, 2013, http://www.bbc.co.uk/
religion/religions/paganism/holydays/beltane_1.shtml.

or rite has a clearly defined role to play. Even if the role is that of an "extra," expectations are at the very least implied, when not defined outright.

The structure of our rituals also reveals a certain continuity throughout the ages: generally beginning with a period of purification, participants then engage in various actions and activities for the purpose of raising the energy of both the masses and the magick to a fever pitch, finally culminating in a climax or "main event" in which the heart of the ritual or rite is expressed and the energy of the working is released to do its best.

Initiation is another element common to many magickal orders past and present. From ancient Greek and Roman initiations into the cults of Isis, Dionysus, and a score of other gods and goddesses, to modern initiations into witchcraft covens such as the Covenant of the Goddess and magickal societies like the Order of the Golden Dawn, initiatory rites have played an important role in the shaping and survival of our Pagan methods, theologies, and group identities for thousands of years.

Although self-initiation is today quite common, many magick workers still feel that only through a more formal initiation can they really consider themselves trained, worthy of following a particular path and certified to dedicate oneself to a patron deity of choice. Perhaps this was a point of influence in ancient times as well; without the wide dissemination of magickal and mystical literature that we have today, initiation into magickal orders and mystery cults was an important, and in many places the only, reliable way to acquire deeper knowledge and understanding of magickal practice and ritual. In modern times, in spite of the ready availability of magickal and mystical information in the form of books, websites, and even videos, we find that some practices and traditions, certain insights and understandings, can only be gained through sharing sacred, mystical, and magickal experiences with others. Just as it was in ancient Greece, so also it is today.

Initiation rituals provide for a structured and controlled entry into mysteries the chaotic depths of which will never be fully charted. As one of magick's most sacred traditions, initiation has paved the way through the ages for cooperative and cohesive spellwork, ritual, and celebration. Although solitary practice can be just as effective as group practice, it's the spells, formulas, techniques, and traditions practiced by *many* that stand the test of time. Offering an outward symbol of the transference of information that occurs between mentor and student, initiation continues in our magickal communities today just as it has in the past, to increase the chances that our magickal techniques and traditions will be appreciated, carried on, and not forgotten.

It's important to note, however, that even when initiation is outwardly something that is given or bestowed by a priest or priestess or the like, true initiation is always a personal, internal and external process which only one's own soul can activate. Although initiatory rites vary greatly from time to time and place to place, there are several elements common to many of these traditions. For example, purification is often an important part of the initiation process. So too do initiates around the world often find themselves facing a trial, or test, of some sort. This aspect is often linked to the purification process, the idea being that after destruction, breakdown, or trial of the soul, a spiritual rebirth becomes possible. Education is yet another element common to many initiations. Whether obtained through direct study of books and other learning materials, or gained through viewing mystically symbolic art, observing ritual reenactments of essential myths, or serving the group in a role akin to an apprentice, initiates-to-be typically receive an education in mysticism and training in the magickal arts.

In looking at the many similarities in group magick of the past and present, one aspect of distinction that stands out is the difference in size between our modern festivals and public rituals and those held by our magickal ancestors. Some of our largest best-known modern Western Pagan gatherings, such as PantheaCon, Pagan Spirit Gathering, and the Saint Louis Pagan Picnic, measure attendance from the high hundreds into the low, single-digit thousands. While these events may be quite fun and festive, they hardly compare to the massive rituals and rites held by some of our Pagan ancestors. One can only imagine the experience of watching a ritual drama at the 17,000-seat Theatre of Dionysus,[160] located at the site of the Acropolis in Athens, Greece, or the thrill of an early European community-wide harvest festival and ritual in which literally everyone in town shows up and plays a role. The sheer size and grandeur of ancient Aztec temples, Egyptian pyramids, and the mysterious Nazca lines make the fact that we get a few witch mentions in the media and put on a handful of well-organized events throughout the year seem like relatively small potatoes in comparison to the mark made by the ancients. While I can't say I envy the Aztecs present at the ritualistic mass slayings of thousands upon thousands of human victims,[161] I do dream of a time when our Pagan group workings become larger and once again truly communal. Perhaps as modern events like our Pagan Pride Day festivals bring our magickal culture further into the spotlight, we'll begin to feel more comfortable singing our Pagan songs a little louder, dancing our ritual dances a little bigger, building our bonfires a little brighter.

Another notable difference between today's magickal groups and those of the past is in the types of magick performed. While personal goals such as wealth, health, beauty, love, and power have for a long while been the rule of the day, magicians past seemed to do quite a lot more magick for the community than we do now. From town-wide spring rituals to the steadfast observance of everyday customs, magickal practice to benefit the good of the community as a whole seems to have been a popular notion and was a prevalent aspect of culture in more "primitive" societies. Yet, we do have our modern equivalents. Practitioners of Global Wicca, for instance, frequently perform Earth-healing magick,[162] while many people who practice the Reclaiming tradition of witchcraft engage in group magick to transform

---

160   See "Theatre of Dionysus," http://www.visit-ancient-greece.com/theatre-of-dionysus.html.

161   See "History of the Aztecs," HistoryWorld.net, http://www.historyworld.net/wrldhis/plaintexthistories.asp?historyid=aa12.

162   See "The Global Wicca Tradition," http://www.globalwicca.com/globalwicca.htm.

societies and governments into a more balanced and harmonious state with the natural world.[163] Everyday folk magicians, your basic non-denominational Pagans, chaos magicians, and any number or variety of other magick workers may also engage in group magick beneficial to the community or the world as a whole. We haven't *totally* forgotten this important use for magick, but it does seem too oft neglected in modern times.

Group Magick Spells

In this chapter, you've seen some examples of how magick workers around the world have used music, dance, specialization, and socializing to make the most of their group rituals. Now let's look at some particular ways you can put group magick to use in your own practice.

Whether practicing solitary or in a group, all your spell options are wide open, of course; there are no restrictions on or distinctions between the types of magick that can be worked alone and the types of magick that can be worked with others. That said, there are certain types of spells you'll find are best when worked with a group. It's of course possible to work such magick on your own, but having a helping hand or two on your side will definitely make these types of spells easier to cast and potentially more effective at half the effort. Here are a few magickal possibilities to explore with your witchy cohorts:

- **Community Magick:** Magick to provide for the needs of the people, whether through a good harvest, a steady rainfall, or protection from enemies, is what community magick is all about. When many of our modern threats assume forms quite different from dangers faced in the past, updating our community magick to reflect our current needs as a society seems like a wise and very necessary step. Observe the needs

---

163   See "The Five-Point Agenda," by Starhawk, http://www.reclaiming.org/about/directions/fivepoint-agenda.html.

and problems of your community, and consider crafting new spells designed to help your town or your planet as a whole. Keep in mind that magick meant to effect the whole community is best cast with the help of other members of that community who share an equal interest in the outcome; select your magickal mates with care and intention. Try group spellcastings to bless your town, state, country, and world. Focus on the provision of necessary resources, the banishing of negative elements, or the manifestation of greater unity and compassion—the possibilities are endless, and with more people to dream, scheme, and spell, the magickal results can achieve truly global proportions.

• **Combining, Joining, and Mixing Magick:** Another type of spellwork that works best with a group is combining, joining, and mixing magick. For example, suppose you want to foster cooperation and positive interaction between two warring nations. If you were casting such a spell alone, it might be a bit difficult to conjure in your mind and heart the essence of warring country "A" while simultaneously conjuring in your mind and heart the essence of warring country "B." With a pal at your side, however, you're free to focus on country "A" while your partner focuses on country "B," making the process a whole lot easier when it comes time to blend and mix the energies together. Whenever the magickal goal is to blend or join together separate energies of various qualities, having others to help with the spell can be very beneficial.

• **Magick Cast Through Sex:** Sexual stimulation can raise tremendous amounts of energy that can be channeled into a wide array of magickal purposes. While you can certainly practice sex magick on your own through focused and intentional self-gratification, it's often more pleasurable to share the experience with another. Having a partner or partners can make it easier to achieve stimulation and raise the necessary energy for the spellwork at hand. Just be sure to not take sex lightly—it's serious business and shouldn't be engaged in without a whole lot of trust and a whole lot of thought, whether you're doing it for magick or simply "doing it."

Overcoming Challenges

While the common motivations and applications for group magick present a picture of harmony, there are indeed many challenges. We've all heard the stories that seem all too familiar, stories of power-trips and jealousies, betrayals and indiscretions, rivalries and hidden agendas that can rip apart even the strongest communities. On top of the most extreme cases, there are also the everyday, relatively minor challenges inherent to group workings. Getting everyone participating at a similar level of intensity and understanding, meshing personalities and unifying very individual traits, beliefs, and powers for a shared and singular magickal purpose can sometimes be quite the uphill battle—I believe the common phrase is "like herding cats."

Another challenge faced by magickal groups far and wide is the seemingly inevitable presence of the disagreeable, dramatic, and antagonistic individual who seems to get in the way of any actual, real magick. Julia Maupin, coven mother for St. Louis area Strawberry Moon Coven, an eclectic Wiccan group, summed up the issue quite well: "I'd have to say the hardest thing about having a group for magick is that sometimes there is just one turd in the punch bowl and eventually you'll have to deal with it. I love all my sisters, brothers, and children but when they start affecting the overall progress of the group, then it's a problem. We made rules and set up discipline, but they are like your family and sometimes you feel like you can't tell them the truth about their attitude or whatever it maybe."

To help overcome these challenges and keep major issues at bay, there are a few techniques group leaders have employed throughout the ages and throughout the world with varying levels of success:

- **Pre-ritual Purification of Participants:** With the aim
  of banishing unwarranted negativity, doubt, and other
  emotionally charged thoughts that could interfere with the
  magickal working, pre-ritual purification is widely practiced
  and fairly standard throughout the world. Methods vary, but
  typical techniques employed for achieving a purified state
  of being include fasting; abstaining from food, sex, or other
  necessary or enjoyable things; anointing the body or bathing
  in sanctified water; fumigation or anointing of the body
  with the smoke or oils of sacred plants; and touching the
  body with ritual implements such as a horn, wand, or pine
  bough. These methods drive unwelcome energies out and
  away from a person before that person enters the ritual site,
  bringing their aura and vibes with them.

- **Pre-ritual Purification of Ritual Space:** Alongside purifying
  ritual participants comes purifying the ritual space. This
  process has the effect of sealing out unwanted energies
  and unwelcome personalities and powers. Many modern
  magicians achieve purification of the ritual space through
  the casting of the magick circle, a method which is quite
  effective when executed with concentration.

- **Exclusivity:** Another way magickal groups have striven to
  keep things cool among themselves is through the exclusion
  of perceived threats to the peace, be they potential challengers
  to the status quo, individuals with ulterior or conflicting
  motives and agendas, or simply those persons deemed as "bad
  influences" by the current society. Such exclusion has ranged
  from age restrictions to gender restrictions. While some
  restrictions might make sense, others seem questionable at
  best and downright prejudice, segregating, and oppressive at
  worst. When considering the exclusion of others from your

magickal group, weigh the decision carefully and take a close look at your motivations. Are your reasons based on fear, or prejudice, or are your reasons wise, and just? Would it really hurt or jeopardize anything to allow others into your group? Why or why not?

- **Oaths:** Oaths are a common means for fostering group loyalty. When group members take oaths of secrecy or oaths of commitment or service to the group, personal biases are more likely to be tempered by overall group needs, and group confidences are more likely to be kept confident. That said, oaths are only meaningful if they're meant!

- **Everyone Plays a Part:** While exclusion is used by some groups as a method of maintaining order, other groups do so through inclusion. Letting everyone play a part can help group workings run smoothly. Including other members of your group in planning and executing your group rituals will help create a sense of group worth, individual voice, and overall unity. When possible, let people choose the roles they will play—we're much more likely to do a good job of it when we're utilizing our individual strengths and acknowledging our personal interests. Be sure to make accommodations for anyone whose participation might otherwise be limited. For instance, try to provide comfortable seating for anyone who can't stand for long periods of time, and make sure newcomers know what to expect and what's expected.

Group Magick Spell for a Better Community

Here's a spell that has the potential to benefit your entire community. Try it with a group of at least three individuals, but preferably with several more.

Begin by deciding on goals for your community. Your community of focus could be your coven, your woods, your town, your state, your country, your biome, or your whole world. Next, think about the individual magickal skills and interests of each person involved in the spellcasting. Play up the abilities of each participant and design the ritual to make best use of their talents. Is there someone in the group who is particularly good at banishing negative energy, for instance? If so, consider crafting a spell that lets this person use that skill to rid your community of violence, or pollution. Is there an individual in the group that's especially fond of the fae? If so, ask them to call on and evoke their faery friends for help with your magick. Is someone in your group a pro at divination? Invite them to do a reading regarding the magickal work at hand, identifying potential trouble spots and hidden opportunities. Decide also who will lead the ritual, and what signals will be used to let the other participants know when it's time to move on to the next part of the casting.

Next, begin the ritual by casting the circle if you like and invoking any desired spirits, energies, deities, etc. Depending on how many folks you have to do the working, divvy up your group into musicians and dancers, or simply give everyone a musical instrument to play while they move their feet, as well. Any instruments can be used, of course, but you might find that you get better results employing different instruments for different purposes. For instance, drums and other percussion instruments are good for magnifying energy and representing power, while wind and string instruments are great for attracting or altering energies. Bells are excellent for banishing negativity, welcoming positivity, causing change, achieving balance, and summoning natural forces.

Have a percussionist set the beat, then let other musicians join in as compelled. As the music builds in intensity, the dancing should also become more energetic. The group can choose to focus as a whole on each community goal in turn, combining their powers by collectively willing desired changes to manifest and envisioning it as being so. Or, your group might choose to employ specialization, with each individual focusing on one particular goal and one particular aspect of the spell. If any of the chosen goals for your community involve getting rid of something, like reducing the number of guns floating around, for instance, you might have the person in your group who is best at banishing beat on a drum or clang a heavy bell with force and intention, envisioning the baneful forces being driven out and away by the raucous sound. If any of the chosen goals for your community involve manifesting, attracting, or increasing something, like ensuring a good harvest, for example, have musicians envision the object of these goals increasing and growing, coming closer and brighter as the music is played. Once intentions are set and energy is at its high, release the spell to do its work. Wrap it up with some socialization—share "cakes and ale," or cookies and juice, as suits your fancy. Talk about your personal lives and/or ritual lives, your worries and challenges, your hopes and your triumphs. As you wrap up the current ritual time knowing the Better Community spell you just cast will succeed, share ideas for future magick to help yourself, your group, and your world as a whole. Both your magickal community and your mundane community will benefit not only from the direct, magickal effects of the present ritual, but also from the increased strength and unity that results when we make the time to make magick with friends.

Points to Ponder

- Have you ever practiced magick with other people? Would you like to have more experiences with group magick? What might you gain from such experiences?

- What do you see as the advantages and disadvantages of group magick? Do the benefits outweigh the ills, in your opinion? Why or why not?

- This chapter discussed initiation rites, ritual structure, and other commonalities between magickal groups both past and present. Can you identify any other points of similarity or distinction you feel are important to note?

- What types of magick do you feel are best practiced alone? Are there any spells that would be better cast in a group setting?

- Do magickal groups and societies foster growth within our Pagan communities? Why or why not? What might such groups do to better nurture the evolution of our culture? Have some groups become too "churchy," too organized and hierarchical for our own good?

- Do you currently belong to any magickal groups? If so, does the group suit you? Why or why not? If you are a solitary, does the idea of having a group of like-minded magick workers with whom to swap ideas and share rituals appeal to you?

- Describe your ideal magick group. Who are the members? What might you do with such a magickal dream team? How would this group improve upon what's been offered in the past? What would be the same, and what would be very different?

Bibliography

Abercromby, John. *Magic Songs of the West Finns, Vol. 2.* London: David Nutt, 1898, 108. Accessed January 3, 2013, http://www.sacred-texts .com/neu/ms2/ms200.htm.

Adams, John Paul. "Dionysos." January 23, 2010. California State University. Accessed March 23, 2013, http://www.csun.edu/~hcfll004/dionysos.html.

Amazulu: The Life of the Zulu Nation. "Zulu Healing." Accessed March 24, 2013, http://library.thinkquest.org/27209/Healing.htm.

Ancient Egypt Online. "Nephthys." Accessed March 13, 2013, http://ancient egyptonline.co.uk/nephthys.html.

Ashforth, Adam. *Witchcraft, Violence, and Democracy in South Africa.* Chicago: University of Chicago Press, 2005, 52-57, 133–142.

Barrett, Francis. *The Magus.* London: Lackington, Alley and Co., 1801. Accessed August 1, 2012, http://www.sacred-texts.com/grim/magus/ma100.htm.

BBC.com. "Beltane." Accessed March 24, 2013, http://www.bbc.co.uk /religion/religions/paganism/holydays/beltane_1.shtml.

Bell, Deborah. *Mask Makers and their Craft: An Illustrated Worldwide Study.* Jefferson, NC: McFarland and Co., 2010, 98–99.

Bloomfield, Maurice, trans. *Hymns of the Atharva-Veda: Sacred Books of the East, Vol. 42.* Oxford, UK: Oxford University Press, 1897, I, 17, "Charm to Stop the Flow of Blood," III, 25, "Charm to Arouse the Passionate Love of a Woman," V, 14, "Charm to Repel Sorceries or Spells," V, 31, "Charm to Repel Sorceries or Spells." Accessed March 28, 2012, http://www.sacred -texts.com/hin/sbe42/av000.htm.

Bonwick, James. *Irish Druids and Old Irish Religions.* London: Griffith, Farran, 1894, 47–48, 50, 51, 61. Accessed June 5, 2012, http://www.sacred -texts.com/pag/idr/idr00.htm.

Borgeaud, Philippe. *Mother of the Gods: From Cybele to the Virgin Mary.* Translated by Lysa Hochroth. Baltimore, MD: The John Hopkins University Press, 2004, 62–66.

Budge, E. A. Wallis. *Egyptian Magic.* London: Kegan, Paul, Trench and Trübner & Co. 1901, 84–85. Accessed March 1, 2012, http://www.sacred-texts .com/egy/ema/ema00.htm.

Callaway, Henry. *The Religious System of the Amazulu.* Springvale, Natal: J. A. Blair, 1870, 443. Accessed January 15, 2012, http://www.sacred-texts .com/afr/rsa/rsa00.htm.

Carmicheal, Alexander. *Carmina Gadelica: Hymns and Incantations, Volume 2.* Edinburgh, UK: T. and A. Constable, 1900, 53. Accessed June 4, 2012, http://www.sacred-texts.com/neu/celt/cg2/index.htm.

CBS News Sunday Morning. "Superstitions: Why You Believe." Accessed February 8, 2013. http://www.cbsnews.com/8301-3445_162-57541783 /superstitions-why-you-believe/

Charkraverty, Somnath, Dr. *Rock Art and Tribal Art of India.* "Bhimbetka: the Glimpses of Indian Rock-Art in a World Heritage Site." Accessed March 23, 2013, http://rockartandtribalartofindia.blogspot .com/2010/07/bhimbetka-glimpses-of-indian-rock-art.html.

Cheema, Sushil. "The Big Dig: The Yanks Uncover a Red Sox Jersey." *The New York Times*, April 14, 2008. Accessed January 5, 2013, http://www.nytimes.com/2008/04/14/sports/baseball/14jersey.html.

Clodd, Edward. *Tom Tit Tot*. London: Duckworth and Company, 1898, "Magic Through Tangible Things," "Words of Power." Accessed March 23, 2013, http://www.sacred-texts.com/neu/celt/ttt/ttt11.htm.

College of New Rochelle. "Companion: Defixiones (Curse Tablets)." Accessed March 1, 2012, http://www2.cnr.edu/home/araia/defixiones.html.

Cutright-Smith, Elisabeth Melitta. "Modeling Ancestral Hopi Agricultural Landscapes." Thesis, Dept. of Anthropology, University of Arizona. Ann Arbor, MI: ProQuest Information and Learning Company, 2007, 84.

De Molina, Christoval. "The Fables and Rites of the Yncas." In *Narratives of the Rites and Laws of the Yncas*, edited and translated by Clements R. Markham. London: Hakluyt Society, 1873, "July," "August." Accessed March 23, 2013, http://www.sacred-texts.com/nam/inca/rly/rly00.htm.

Edkins, Rev. Joseph, DD. *Chinese Buddhism: a Volume of Sketches, Historical, Descriptive, and Critical*. London: Kegan Paul, Trench, Trübner and Company, 1893, 387. Accessed January 5, 2012, http://openlibrary.org/books/OL23286290M/Chinese_Buddhism.

Edwards, William Howell. *An Introduction to Aboriginal Societies*. South Melbourne, AU: Social Science Press, 2004, 80.

Ellis, A. B. *Yoruba-Speaking Peoples of the Slave Coast of West Africa*. 1894. Reprint, Charleston, SC: Forgotten Books, 2007, 97–98.

Ellis, Peter Berresford. *A Brief History of the Druids*. New York: Carroll and Graf Publishers, 2002, 59–60.

Elworthy, Frederick Thomas. *The Evil Eye: An Account of this Ancient and Widespread Superstition*. London: J. Murray, 1895, 53–58, 82. Accessed February 15, 2012, http://www.sacred-texts.com/evil/tee/tee00.htm.

Enotes.com. "Australian Aborigines." Accessed March 23, 2013, http://www
.enotes.com/australian-aborigines-reference/australian-aborigines.

Face Music. "Traditional Instruments of the Uganda People." "Traditional
Dance of the Uganda People." Accessed March 23, 2013, http://www.face-
music.ch/instrum/uganda_instrumen.html, http://www.face-music.ch
/instrum/uganda_danceen.html.

Faulkner, R. O. *The Ancient Egyptian Pyramid Texts*. 1969. Reprint, Stilwell: Digireads.com, 2007, 86.

Fergusson, Erna. *Dancing Gods: Indian Ceremonials of New Mexico and Arizona*. New York: Alfred A. Knopf, 1931, 122, 131–132. Accessed March
23, 2013, http://www.sacred-texts.com/nam/sw/dg/.

Frazer, Sir James George. *The Golden Bough*. 1922. Reprint, New York: Bar-
tleby.com, 2000, chapter 5, section 4, "The Magical Control of the Wind,"
chapter 3, section 3, "Contagious Magic," chapter 34, "The Myth and Ritual of Attis." Accessed January 9, 2012, http://www.bartleby.com/196/.

Gager, John G., ed. *Curse Tablets and Binding Spells from the Ancient World*.
New York: Oxford University Press, 1992, 18–19, 34, 95.

Gallop, Rodney. "A Pagan Cult Survives in Mexico." *Discovery: A Popular Journal of Knowledge, New Series*, Vol. 2, No. 10 (1939): 218–227.

Geary, Theresa Flores, PhD. *The Illustrated Bead Bible: Terms, Tips, and
Techniques*. New York: Sterling Publishing Co., Inc., 2008, 115.

Georgia Writer's Project, Savannah Unit. Mary Granger, District Supervisor. *Drums and Shadows*. Athens, GA: University of Georgia Press, 1940,
"Tin City," 12, "Sunbury," 111. Accessed May 15, 2012, http://www.sacred
-texts.com/afr/das/das00.htm.

Greenfield, Richard P. H. "Evil Eye." In *Encyclopedia of Ancient Greece*,
edited by Nigel Wilson, 284–285. New York: Routledge, 2006.

Grey, Sir George. *Polynesian Mythology and Ancient Traditional History of the New Zealanders: As Furnished by Their Priests and Chiefs.* London: John Murray, 1855, 125–126, 200–203. Accessed March 23, 2013, http://www.sacred-texts.com/pac/grey/grey00.htm.

Haikal, Fayza. "The Mother's Heart, the Hidden Name, and True Identity: Paternal/Maternal Descent and Gender Dichotomy." In *Echoes of Eternity: Studies Presented to Gaballa Aly Gaballa,* edited by Ola El-Aguizy and Mohamed Sherif Ali, 197. Wiesbaden, DE: Otto Harrassowitz Verlag, 2010.

Handwerk, Brian. "'Python Cave' Reveals Oldest Human Ritual, Scientists Suggest." *National Geographic News,* December 22, 2006. Accessed August 1, 2012, http://news.nationalgeographic.com/news/2006/12/061222-python-ritual.html.

Hansen, Chadwick. Excerpt from *Witchcraft at Salem.* New York: G. Braziller, 1969. In *The Salem Witch Trials Reader,* edited by Francis Hill, 233–245. Cambridge, MA: Da Capo Press, 2000.

Hanson, Glen, Peter Venturelli, and Annette Fleckenstein. *Drugs and Society.* Sudbury, MA: Jones and Bartlett Publishers, LLC, 2009, 327.

Harrison, Jane. *Ancient Art and Ritual.* London: Thornton Butterworth LTD, 1913, 31–32. Accessed March 3, 2012, http://www.sacred-texts.com/cla/aar/aar00.htm.

Heliodorus. *Æthiopica.* Translated passage in *The Gnostics and Their Remains,* by Charles William King (London: David Nutt, 1887), 195. Accessed February 1, 2012, http://www.sacred-texts.com/gno/gar/gar00.htm.

HistoryWorld.net. "History of the Aztecs." Accessed March 23, 2013, http://www.historyworld.net/wrldhis/plaintexthistories.asp?historyid=aa12.

Hoffman, W. J., MD. "Folk-Lore of the Pennsylvania Germans, Part II." *Journal of American Folk-Lore,* 2:4 (1889): 23–35. Accessed May 5, 2012, http://www.sacred-texts.com/ame/fpg/fpg00.htm.

Hohman, John George. *Long Lost Friend* . 1820. Trans., Camden, UK: Star and Book Novelty Company, 1828, "Another Remedy to be Applied when Anyone is Sick," "Another Method of Making Cattle Return Home," "A Good Remedy Against Calumniation or Slander." Accessed March 23, 2013, http://www.sacred-texts.com/ame/pow/pow000.htm.

Horan, Kevin. "William Penn Atop Philly Once Again." MLB.com, October 3, 2008. Accessed January 10, 2012, http://mlb.mlb.com/news/article. jsp?ymd=20081027&content_id=3648489&vkey=ps2008news&fext =jsp&c_id=mlb.

Illes, Judika. *Encyclopedia of Spirits*. New York: Harper Collins Publishers, 2009, 611–612.

Joralemon, Peter David. "The Olmec." In *The Face of Ancient America: The Wally and Brenda Zollman Collection of Precolumbian Art*, edited by Lee A. Parsons, John B. Carlson, and Peter David Joralemon. Indianapolis, IN: Indianapolis Museum of Art, 1988, 9–50.

Lawerence, Robert Means. *The Magic of the Horse-Shoe With Other Folk-Lore Note*. Cambridge: The Riverside Press, 1898, chapter VI, "Iron as a Protective Charm." Accessed August 1, 2012, http://www.sacred-texts .com/etc/mhs/mhs00.htm.

Leary, Robert. "Women on the Mountain: Exploring the Dionysiac Mysteries." Thesis presented to Ohio University, 2010. Accessed March 23, 2013, at http://etd.ohiolink.edu/send-pdf.cgi/Leary%20Robert .pdf?ouhonors1282940703.

Leland, Charles Godfrey. *Gypsy Sorcery and Fortune Telling*. London: T. Fisher Unwin, 1891, 95, 110–111, 120–121. Accessed January 2, 2012, http://www.sacred-texts.com/pag/gsft/gsft00.htm.

Lin, Joseph. "The Curse of the Bambino." In "Top 10 Sports Superstitions." Time.com, October 19, 2011. Accessed January 5, 2013, http:// keepingscore.blogs.time.com/2011/10/19/top-10-sports-superstitions /slide/curse-of-the-bambino/.

MacCulloch, John Arnott. *The Religion of the Ancient Celts.* 1911. Repr., Charleston, SC: BiblioBazaar, LLC, 2006, 196.

Macdonald, James. *Religion and Myth.* London: David Nutt; New York: Scribner, 1883, 104–105. Accessed May 5, 2012, http://www.sacred-texts .com/afr/ram/ram00.htm.

Mackenzie, Donald A. *Myths of Crete and Pre-Hellenic Europe.* 1917. Reprint, Whitefish, MT: Kessinger Publishing, 2004, 53.

Massey, Dr. Alan. "The Reigate Witch Bottle." *Current Archeology*, no. 169 (2000): 34–36.

McGrory, Brian. "Taking Teeth Out of Curse? Teen Hit by Ramirez Foul Ball Lives in Babe Ruth's Former House." *The Boston Globe*, September 2, 2004. On Boston.com. Accessed January 5, 2013, http://www.boston.com /news/local/articles/2004/09/02/taking_teeth_out_of_curse/?page=full.

McManus, Barbara F. "Background and Images for the Bacchae." 1999. Accessed March 23, 2013, http://www2.cnr.edu/home/bmcmanus /bacchaebg.html.

Menen, Rajendar. *The Healing Power of Mudras.* New Delhi: V&S Publishers, 2011, 12.

Mercer, Samuel A. B., trans. *The Pyramid Texts.* New York, London, Toronto: Longmans, Green, and Co., 1952, Utterance 241, Utterance 293, Utterance 534. Accessed January 1, 2013, http://www.sacred-texts.com/egy /pyt/pyt00.htm.

Moore, A. W. *Folk-Lore of the Isle of Man.* London: D. Nutt, 1891, 76. Accessed June 1, 2012, http://www.sacred-texts.com/neu//celt/fim/fim00.htm.

Nassau, Rev. Robert Hamill. *Fetichism in West Africa.* 1904. Reprint, Charleston, SC: BiblioBazaar, LLC, 2008, 75–76.

"Nazar Boncugu or Turkish Evil Eye Bead Amulets." Accessed March 11, 2013, http://www.nazarboncugu.com/.

Oettinger, Marion, Jr. *Folk Treasure of Mexico: The Nelson A. Rockefeller Collection.* Houston, TX: Arte Publico Press, 2012, 35.

Official Website of Switzerland Tourism. MySwitzerland.com. "Fastnacht in Basel (BS)." Accessed March 23, 2013, http://www.myswitzerland .com/en/fasnacht-in-basel-bs.html.

Ogden, Daniel. "Binding Spells: Curse Tablets and Voodoo Dolls in the Greek and Roman Worlds." In *Witchcraft and Magic in Europe, Volume 2: Ancient Greece and Rome,* edited by Bengt Ankarloo and Stuart Clark, 6, 12, 14. Philadelphia: University of Pennsylvania Press, 1999.

———. *Magic, Witchcraft, and Ghosts in the Greek and Roman Worlds: A Sourcebook.* New York: Oxford University Press, 2002, 212.

Parker, Arthur C. *The Code of Handsome Lake, the Seneca Prophet.* Albany, NY: University of the State of New York, 1913, 122–123, "Society of Mystic Animals," 124–125, "The Eagle Society," 129, "Key to Phonetic System." Accessed March 23, 2013, http://www.sacred-texts.com/nam/iro /parker/cohl000.htm.

Phipps, Elena. *Cochineal Red: The Art History of a Color.* New York: Metropolitan Museum of Art, 2010, 24.

Pocs, Eva. "Curse, Maleficium, Divination: Witchcraft on the Borderline of Religion and Magic." In *Witchcraft Continued: Popular Magic in Modern Europe,* edited by Willem De Blécourt and Owen Davies. Manchester, UK: Manchester University Press, 2004, 174–190.

Pool, Christopher A. *Olmec Archaeology and Early Mesoamerica.* Cambridge: Cambridge University Press, 2007, 173–174.

Pyramid Texts Online. Accessed January 1, 2013, http://www.pyramid-textsonline.com/.

Ralston, W. E. S., MA. *Songs of the Russian People.* London: Ellis and Green, 1872, 358–359, 365, 369. Accessed May 7, 2012, http://www.sacred-texts. com/neu/srp/srp00.htm.

Rätsch, Christian. *Marijuana Medicine: A World Tour of the Healing and Visionary Powers of Cannabis.* 1998. Repr., Rochester, VT: Inner Traditions International, 2001, 16–18.

Religious Facts. "Big Religion Chart." Accessed February 10, 2013, http://www.religionfacts.com/big_religion_chart.htm.

Rink, Henry. *Tales and Traditions of the Eskimo.* Edinburgh, London: William, Blackwood, and Sons, 1875, 52–53. Accessed April 4, 2012, http://www.sacred-texts.com/nam/inu/tte/tte0-0.htm.

Robinson, Scott R. Robinson. "Origins of Theatre." Central Washington University. Accessed March 23, 2013, http://www.cwu.edu/~robinsos/ppages/resources/Theatre_History/Theahis_1.html.

Roth, Walter E. Roth. "An Inquiry into the Animism and Folk-lore of the Guiana Indians." In *The Thirtieth Annual Report of the Bureau of American Ethnology, 1908–1909,* Chapter VIII, "The Spirits of the Bush," section 109, "Why the Drink Turned Sour." Washington, D.C.: Bureau of American Ethnology, 1915. Accessed June 1, 2012, http://www.sacred-texts.com/nam/sa/aflg/aflg000.htm.

Rousselot, Jean-Loup. "Yupik and Inupiaq Masks (Alaska)." In *Shamanism: An Encyclopedia of World Beliefs, Practices, and Culture, Volume I,* edited by Mariko Namba Walter, Eva Jane Neumann Fridman. Santa Barbara: ABC-CLIO Inc., 2004, 358–361.

Ryan, Marah Ellis. *Pagan Prayers.* Chicago: A.C. McClurg and Company, 1913, "Prayer of Transformation into a Lotus." Accessed March 23, 2013, http://www.sacred-texts.com/pag/ppr/ppr00.htm.

Scott, Florence Johnson. "Customs and Superstitions among Texas Mexicans on the Rio Grande Border." In *Coffee in the Gourd,* edited by J. Frank Dobie, section IV, "Omens and Superstitions." Austin, TX: Texas Folklore Society, 1923. Accessed February 1, 2012, http://www.sacred-texts.com/ame/cig/cig00.htm.

Sebald, Hans. "Shaman, Healer, Witch: Comparing Shamanism with Franconian Folk Magick." 1984. Repr. in *Witchcraft, Healing, and Popular Diseases: New Perspectives on Witchcraft, Magic, and Demonology, Vol. 5*, edited by Brian P. Levack. New York: Routledge, 2001, 309–326.

Shaughnessy, Dan. *Reversing the Curse: Inside the 2004 Boston Red Sox.* New York: Houghton Mifflin Company, 2005, 231.

Shortland, Edward. *Maori Religion and Mythology.* London: Longmans, Green, and Co., 1882, 35. Accessed February 2, 2012, http://www.sacred-texts.com/pac/mrm/mrm00.htm.

Simons, Patricia. *The Sex of Men in Premodern Europe: A Cultural History.* Cambridge, UK: Cambridge University Press, 2011, 53.

Smith, Michael E. "Aztecs." In *The Oxford Handbook of the Archaeology of Ritual and Religion*, edited by Timothy Insoll. New York: Oxford University Press, 2011, 556–570.

Spicer, Dorothy Gladys. *Festivals of Western Europe.* New York: H.W. Wilson Company, 1958, Section 12, "Festivals of Switzerland." Accessed March 23, 2013, http://www.sacred-texts.com/etc/fwe/fwe00.htm.

Starhawk. "The Five-Point Agenda." Reclaiming.org. 1995. Accessed March 23, 2013, http://www.reclaiming.org/about/directions/five-point-agenda.html.

Stark, Rodney. *Discovering God: The Origins of the Great Religions and the Evolution of Belief.* New York: Harper Collins, 2007, 137–139.

Sterckx, Roel. *The Animal and the Daemon in Early China.* Albany, NY: State University of New York Press, 2002, 188.

Summers, Montague. *The Vampire: His Kith and Kin.* London: K. Paul Trench, Trubner, 1928, 148, 328. Accessed February 14, 2013, http://www.sacred-texts.com/goth/vkk/vkk00.htm.

Summers-Effler, Erika. "Ritual Theory." In *Handbook of the Sociology of Emotions*, edited by Jan E. Stets and Jonathan H. Turner, 135–153. New York: Springer Science + Business Media, 2007.

Talbot, D. Amaury. *Woman's Mysteries of a Primitive People.* London: Cassell and Company, LTD., 1915, 174-175. Accessed November 12, 2012, http://www.sacred-texts.com/afr/wmp/wmp00.htm.

"Theatre of Dionysus." Visit-Ancient-Greece.com. Accessed March 23, 2013, http://www.visit-ancient-greece.com/theatre-of-dionysus.html.

The Ancient Egypt Site. "The Pyramid Complex of Unas." Accessed January 1, 2013, http://www.ancient-egypt.org/index.html.

"The Global Wicca Tradition." GlobalWicca.com. Accessed March 23, 2013, http://www.globalwicca.com/globalwicca.htm.

The World Botanical Associates. "Acalypha." Accessed March 3, 2013, http://www.worldbotanical.com/acalypha.htm.

Thiselton-Dyer, T. F. *Folk-Lore of Women.* Chicago: A.C. McClurg and Co., London: Elliot Stock, 1906, Chapter XXIII. Accessed May 1, 2012, http://www.sacred-texts.com/wmn/fow/fow00.htm.

Thomas, W. Jenkyn. *The Welsh Fairy Book.* 1908. Reprint, Charleston, SC: BiblioBazaar, LLC, 2008, 167.

Trachtenberg, Joshua. *Jewish Magic and Superstition.* New York: Behrman's Jewish Book House, 1939, 115–116, 122–123, 123–124. Accessed January 11, 2012, http://www.sacred-texts.com/jud/jms/jms00.htm.

Usma, John. "Reversing the Curse: Red Sox Jersey Excavated from Yankee Stadium." COEDMagazine.com, April 14, 2008. Accessed January 5, 2013, http://coedmagazine.com/2008/04/14/reversing-the-curse-red-sox-jersey-excavated-at-yankee-stadium/.

Van den Dugan, Wim. "The Pyramid Texts of Unas: The Royal Ritual of Rebirth and Illumination." Accessed January 1, 2013, http://maat.sofiatopia.org/wenis_text.htm#XII.

Varner, Gary R. *The History and Use of Amulets, Charms, and Talismans.* Raleigh, NC: Lulu.com, 2008, 36–37.

West, E.W., trans. *Pahlavi Texts, Part III, Sacred Books of the East, Volume 24.* New York: Clarendon, Oxford University Press, 1885, 270. Accessed May 9, 2012, http://www.sacred-texts.com/zor/sbe24/sbe24000.htm.

Wilde, Lady Francesca Speranza. *Ancient Legends, Mystic Charms, and Superstitions of Ireland.* London: Ward & Downey, 1887, "A Love Potion." Accessed March 23, 2013, http://www.sacred-texts.com/neu/celt/ali/ali000.htm.

Williams, Joseph J. *Voodoos and Obeahs: Phases of West India Witchcraft.* New York: Lincoln Mac Veagh, Dial Press Inc., 1932, 152–153. Accessed March 23, 2013, http://www.sacred-texts.com/afr/vao/vao00.htm.

Willoughby, Harold R. *Pagan Regeneration: A Study of Mystery Initiations in the Graeco-Roman World.* Chicago: University of Chicago Press, 1929, Chapter II. Accessed March 23, 2013, http://www.sacred-texts.com/cla/pr/pr00.htm.

Winduo, Steven Edmund. "Indigenous Knowledge of Medicinal Plants in Papau New Guinea." Paper presented to the Macmillan Brown Center for Pacific Studies, 2006, 15. Accessed March 15, 2013. http://www.pacs.canterbury.ac.nz/documents/Steven%20Winduo%20Macmillan%20Brown%20Seminar.pdf.

Winstedt, R. O. *Shaman, Saiva, and Sufi: A Study of the Evolution of Malay Magic.* Glasgow, UK: The University Press, 1925, chapter IV, "The Malay Charm." Accessed March 9, 2012. http://www.sacred-texts.com/sha/sss/sss00.htm.

Index

– A –

Aboriginal, 189

Acropolis, 194

addiction, 77

Africa, 9, 30, 31, 60, 114, 115, 191

African-Americans, 130

afterlife, 52, 142

Agni, 147

Ahura Mazda, 72

Alaska, 168, 169

Amazon, 114

America, 9, 112–114, 127, 169, 171, 181

American folk magick, 14

amulets, 59–62, 82, 116, 117

animal, 14, 31, 86, 117, 124, 132, 146, 168, 169, 172, 186, 189, 190

animal mask, 168

Arabic, 14, 15, 99

Asia, 9, 116, 148, 187

Asia Minor, 187

Athens, 130, 134, 194

Ausar, 52

Australia, 86

Austria, 23

– B –

Baganda, 114, 115

banish, 19, 42, 118

Basel, 174

bells, 27, 126, 127, 173, 200

Beltane, 191

Bhimbetka rock shelters, 189

bind, 41, 42, 69, 70, 73–78, 82, 83, 91

binding magick, 78, 156

binding spell, 83, 84

binding tablets, 81

blood, 17, 39, 112, 117, 119, 140, 187

body-derived ingredients, 44, 60, 104, 109, 127, 128, 130–132, 146, 149, 157

bodily fluids, 133

body magick, 7–9, 23, 24, 27, 28

body movement magick, 22

bones, 18, 20, 60, 144, 147, 148, 188

Botswana, 2

bottle, 59, 112, 118, 120, 123, 127, 131, 133

box, 56, 59

breaking, 14, 43, 124, 125, 127, 135, 136, 149, 156–159

bronze, 83

Brujería, 85

burning, 3, 90, 135, 147

burns, 14, 19, 25, 90

burying, 57, 85, 135

– C –

Carib string puzzle, 113, 118

cattle, 31, 58, 70

Central America, 9

China, 168

Christian, 15, 39, 91

Christianity, 1, 19

claws, 60, 191

clay, 84, 90, 92–94, 134, 171

clothing, 48, 76, 163, 169, 176, 179

coffin, 51–53, 56

combining magick, 42, 49, 95

community, 130, 133, 134, 174, 181–186, 189–191, 194–196, 199–201

confidence, 21, 46, 94

conjure, 12, 26, 130, 134, 135, 147, 156, 196

contagion principle, 62, 63, 123

containing magick, 51, 53, 54, 57, 59, 60, 62–64, 67, 69, 71, 95

copper, 84

corp chreadh, 84, 85

costumes, 163–169, 171–178

counteractive magick, 143, 150

countercharm, 35, 131, 132, 146–148, 156, 157, 160

countercurse, 138, 139, 160

countermagick, 135, 145, 146, 150, 154, 156–160

counter-spell, 146

courage, 32, 49, 78, 176

coven, 183, 197, 199

crops, 10, 24, 25, 163, 165, 185, 186

crossroads, 39

crystal, 3, 61, 64, 65, 94

curse, 10, 11, 14, 19, 34, 37, 81–84, 94, 98, 111, 112, 118–127, 129, 131–158

cursebreaking, 111, 126, 129–133, 135, 136, 138, 139, 141, 142, 144–151, 153, 155–161

curse object, 133–135, 146

Curse of the Bambino, 135, 144, 145

Curse Victim Diagnostic Checklist, 151

cursing, 11, 82, 85, 129, 136, 152, 156, 160

– D –

dance, 23, 24, 119, 126, 164–168, 172, 175, 178, 188, 189, 191, 195

dancing, 23, 24, 27, 160, 163–166, 184, 186, 187, 194, 200

Dawando`, 190

Day of the Dead, 172

dead, 52, 53, 55, 103, 114, 142, 171–173, 176

death, 31, 34, 39, 52, 55, 84, 102, 103, 114, 171–174

deathmaker, 86

decoy, 111–114, 116–131, 133

decoy magick, 111–114, 117, 118, 122, 124–130

decoy object, 118, 121–126

decoy principle, 111, 112, 116, 119, 120, 122, 127, 128

defense, 45, 46, 78, 79, 83, 145

defixiones, 81, 82

Demeter, 42, 43

demon, 54, 56, 63, 113, 148

demon-trapping, 53

depression, 10, 46, 153

Dionysian, 185, 186, 188

Dionysians, 184, 188

Dionysus, 184–187, 192, 194

dirt, 39, 57, 65, 104, 115, 165

disease, 10, 31, 148, 173, 174

doll, 84, 85, 94, 124, 134, 135, 156, 167

drama, 163, 166, 174–176, 178, 188, 189, 191, 194

drink, 20, 21, 30, 33, 35, 36, 42–44, 48, 49, 74, 114, 130

Druids, 21–23, 57, 58, 61

drumming, 172

– E –

egg, 32, 61, 131

Egypt, 22, 51, 99, 100, 103, 116, 117, 141–143

Eleusinian Mysteries, 42

Eleusinian Passion Play, 174, 175

enemy, 40, 57, 67, 69, 76–78, 82, 85, 86, 92, 101, 102, 104, 105, 130, 134, 138, 142, 143, 154–156, 158

energetic signature, 36, 48, 97, 104, 112, 131–133

England, 1, 61, 86, 112, 127, 132

Europe, 9, 23, 70, 82–85, 98, 116, 138, 173, 185

evil eye, 9–11, 14, 18, 26, 86, 116, 117, 131

exorcism, 100, 113, 118, 119, 127, 168

eye, 9–11, 14, 18, 19, 26, 86, 116–118, 123, 131, 134, 172, 177

eye beads, 116–118, 123

– F –

face paint, 172

Fastnacht, 173, 174

fattura della morte, 86

feathers, 166, 168, 178

figurine, 87

fingernails, 109, 112, 130, 131

Finnish, 72, 101, 102

flax, 23, 24, 45, 57

flutes, 188

folk magick, 14, 15, 19, 140

food, 30–32, 34–36, 42–44, 48, 49, 54, 55, 65, 137, 138, 167, 169, 198

footprint, 86, 87

fruit, 86

– G –

garlic, 14, 41, 42

garment, 136

Georgia, 106, 130, 133, 134

Germany, 14, 23, 86, 140

ghost, 15, 51, 54–56, 63–65, 114, 116, 120

glass, 64, 86, 116, 141

Good Eye, 11, 26

good luck, 32, 39, 63

grave, 38, 39, 52, 57, 63, 114, 116

Greco-Roman, 81, 187

Greece, 10, 14, 82–84, 98, 174, 184, 185, 191, 192, 194

Greek, 9, 11, 82–84, 98, 99, 174, 175, 181, 184, 191, 192

group magick, 181–184, 188, 190, 193–195, 197, 199, 201

– H –

hair, 35, 36, 48, 76, 97, 104–107, 109, 112, 117, 120, 123, 124, 127, 130, 132, 133, 147, 156, 157, 164

harvest, 165, 184, 194, 195, 201

healing, 14, 15, 24, 30, 32, 49, 59, 88, 91, 99, 129, 132, 133, 140, 151, 157, 167, 168

hemp, 23, 24, 90

herbal mixtures, 30

herbs, 7, 8, 14, 24, 32, 34, 37, 38, 95

Hindu, 17, 24, 89, 90, 142, 143

honey, 33, 46, 47

Hopi, 163, 165

horn, 14, 198

horns, 60, 168

Hungarians, 138

Husk Faces, 190

– I –

Ibibio, 54–56

identification, 97–102, 104–109, 128, 148, 168

idiong, 54, 55

image magick, 84

imitative act, 86, 92, 133

imitative action, 57, 133

imitative actions, 24, 59

imitative magick, 30, 57, 59, 84, 132

Incas, 169

India, 56, 116, 143, 189

Indra, 147

initiation, 192, 193, 201

insertion, 81, 85–88, 91–95

insertion magick, 81, 88, 91, 93, 95

Inuit, 61, 62

inyangas, 30

Ireland, 37, 57

Irish, 21, 22, 37, 57, 58, 61

iron, 14, 54, 83, 92, 94, 112

Iroquois, 166, 167

Isis, 103, 192

Italy, 14, 86

– J –

Jamaica, 55

jampis, 16

jar, 51, 54, 65

Jewish, 32, 33, 40, 99

jinn, 14

– K –

Kenya, 112

knot, 69–79

knots, 69–79, 113

knot magick, 69–71, 73, 75–77, 79

– L –

lead, 34, 81, 83, 118, 139, 142, 143, 154, 158, 200

London, 10, 12, 13, 15, 20–23, 34, 35, 37, 41, 53, 55, 57, 58, 61, 62, 71, 73–75, 82, 86, 87, 100, 101, 103, 112, 113, 115, 117, 137, 142, 169, 170

love, 7, 26, 35–38, 43, 45, 46, 74, 75, 77, 84, 88–91, 95, 104, 107, 111, 117, 119, 120, 122, 154, 190, 194, 197

love-charms, 74

love magick, 75

love potion, 35–38

love spell, 37, 88, 104, 111, 120, 122

– M –

machinery, 10, 25

Madagascar, 115

Malay, 16, 88–91, 148, 149

Malaysian, 16

Maori, 136, 137

Marave, 115

mask, 167–169, 171, 172, 176–179

masks, 163, 166, 168, 169, 171–174, 176, 179

maskettes, 171

masquerade, 118, 163, 165, 166, 168, 170, 171, 174–176, 179

maternal lineage, 99, 105

Mecklenburg, 86

meditation, 159, 172

Mediterranean, 82

Megalesia, 187

Mexican, 38, 39, 131

Mexico, 9, 39, 85, 164–166, 171–173

Mictecacihuatl, 39

Middle East, 9, 116

milagros, 39

mimetic action, 174

mimetic movement, 165

mimicry, 24, 25, 163, 174–176, 178, 179, 186

mirror, 64, 65, 141, 142, 144, 145

mixing magick, 29–31, 35, 36, 40, 44, 48, 49, 51, 132, 196

Mother of the Gods, 186–188

mudras, 24

music, 113, 119, 184–189, 191, 195, 200, 201

muthi, 30, 31

– N –

Nagum Boiken, 36

nail clippings, 97, 104, 112, 123

nails, 81–86, 92, 95, 106, 112, 130, 133

name, 14, 15, 54, 55, 77, 86, 93, 97–105, 107, 108, 122, 130, 136, 137, 156

names, 32, 33, 82, 97, 98, 102–104, 106, 108, 187

Naples, 86

naualli, 172

needle, 87

Nephthys, 103

New England, 132

New Zealand, 136

Nigeria, 54

Nivasi, 41, 42

North-Germanic, 14, 15, 17, 19

Nuo, 168

– O –

Olmec, 171, 172

onde, 60, 61

origin, 3, 42, 62, 97, 101, 102, 104, 105, 108, 141, 142, 148, 149, 186

– P –

Papau New Guinea, 36

Papier-mâché, 177

Pennsylvania Dutch, 58, 59, 143, 158

Pennsylvania Germans, 114, 115

Persephone, 174

Philadelphia, 82–84, 98, 139

Phrygia, 184, 187

pin, 85, 86, 98

pins, 84–86, 95, 112

plant, 31, 35, 37, 86

plants, 24, 30, 32, 36, 44, 105, 125, 198

Polynesia, 34

poppets, 81

potion, 29–31, 33, 35–40, 42–44, 47–49

potion making, 29, 30, 44

Powanu, 163, 165

powder, 31, 122, 155, 156

property, 9, 58, 60, 61, 134, 146

protection, 14, 15, 26, 39, 45, 52, 60, 61, 92, 103, 105, 112, 121, 124, 125, 186, 195

Ptah, 52

Ptah-Seker-Ausar figures, 52

puncturing, 81–95

puncturing magick, 86, 87

Pyramid of Unas, 22, 142

Python Rock, 2, 3

– R –

rattles, 164, 188

Red Sox, 135, 136, 144, 145

reflection principle, 141, 142, 145, 148, 149, 159

Rhino Cave, 2, 3

Rio Grande, 10, 11, 38, 131

river, 85, 134, 135

Roma, 35, 36, 40, 70, 73–75, 78, 87

Romania, 138

Romanian, 138

Rome, 82–84, 98, 99, 187

Russia, 23

– S –

sacred girdle, 72, 73

sacrifice, 117, 124, 139, 170

saliva, 48, 109, 112, 123, 131, 132, 147

salt, 13, 40, 41, 46, 58, 64, 157

Sandfly, 134

San Pablito, 85

Santa Muerte, 39

Savannah, 106, 130, 134

Saxons, 23

Scottish, 18, 19, 84, 85

Scotland, 18, 61, 70, 71

sea, 18, 40, 57, 58, 70, 71, 94, 148

Seker, 52

Seneca, 166, 167, 190

serpent, 61, 100, 101

serpent's egg, 61

serrat, 62

shaman, 16, 89, 90, 140, 148, 149, 168, 169, 172

sharp objects, 84, 112, 133

shells, 56, 60, 178, 188

sinking, 135, 153

situa festival, 170

skin, 30, 40, 49, 101, 108, 130, 131, 144, 153, 165, 168

Slavic, 12, 13, 20

South Africa, 30, 31

South America, 113, 169

South Pacific islands, 56

specialization, 182, 189, 190, 195, 200

spell, 4, 7, 8, 14, 15, 18, 21, 24, 25,

27, 32, 33, 37, 40, 42, 49, 51, 53, 59, 62–65, 67, 76–79, 82–85, 88–93, 95, 97–99, 101, 104–108, 111, 118–128, 132–137, 139–143, 146–148, 150, 155–157, 159, 160, 168, 176, 182, 195, 196, 199–201

spells, 4, 8, 11, 12, 25, 27, 30, 32, 44, 57, 63, 64, 73, 82–85, 91, 92, 95, 98, 111, 118, 121, 124, 127, 129, 141–143, 146–149, 159, 160, 182, 193, 195, 196, 202

spell diversion, 111, 122, 124, 125, 127

spell recall, 111, 124, 125, 127

spirit, 12, 21, 27, 31, 32, 36, 38, 42, 45, 54–56, 59–61, 64, 65, 98, 108, 113, 114, 116, 118–120, 125, 149, 155, 168, 169, 172, 173, 176, 193

spirit animal, 172

stick, 60, 63, 88, 93, 94, 113, 119

stones, 2, 7, 8, 24, 85, 86, 104, 105, 109, 114–116, 125, 178

storm, 40, 57, 58, 107

substitute, 103, 117, 120–124

Sunbury, 133, 134

susto, 38

Swabia, 23

Switzerland, 173, 174

symbol, 4, 33, 47, 74, 121–124, 169, 176, 193

sympathetic magick, 62, 85, 87, 90, 92, 95, 123

– T –

talisman, 51, 60, 61, 63, 65, 66, 79, 106

taoist, 53, 56

Tenochtitlan, 188

Texas, 10, 11, 38, 131

Texas Mexicans, 11, 38, 131

Tezcatlipoca, 188

thief, 69, 73, 74

thorns, 81, 86, 95, 112, 133

Thrace, 184

thread, 8, 48, 71, 77, 88

thumb, 21, 23

Tin City, 130

toenails, 130, 131

trance, 24, 172, 187

transference, 87–89, 91–93, 132, 193

transformation, 39, 45, 46, 87–89, 91, 94, 102, 163, 164, 172

Transylvania, 138

Transylvanian, 23

twisted, 70, 78, 79, 106, 114, 157

twisting, 114, 118

– U –

Uganda, 188

umsizi, 31

US, 4, 8, 9, 26, 29, 33, 35, 55, 81,
  87, 104, 106, 108, 111, 129, 135,
  136, 141, 147, 150, 158, 173,
  176, 182, 189, 191

urine, 112, 120, 123, 127, 132, 133

– V –

voice, 11, 15, 16, 25, 33, 106,
  186, 199

– W –

Wales, 61

Wanika, 112, 113, 118, 119, 127

war, 170, 173, 174

water, 20, 29, 33, 40–43, 48, 59,
  64, 85, 94, 131, 132, 143, 157,
  190, 198

water well, 82, 98, 147, 148

Welsh, 69, 70, 78

West Africa, 9, 60

William Penn Curse, 139

willow knot, 74–76

wind, 70–72, 76, 137, 185, 200

witch's bottle, 112, 118, 120, 123,
  127, 131, 133

wisdom, 32, 37, 44, 45, 49, 72

word charms, 12, 14, 15, 17, 18,
  21, 25

– Y –

Yahuayra festivals, 169

Yankees, 135, 136, 144

Yoruba, 60, 61

Yupik, 168, 169

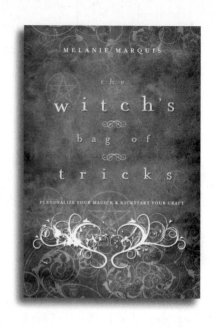

MELANIE MARQUIS

the
witch's
bag of
tricks

PERSONALIZE YOUR MAGICK & KICKSTART YOUR CRAFT

The Witch's Bag of Tricks
Personalize Your Magick & Kickstart Your Craft
Melanie Marquis

Increase your power, improve your spellcasting, and reclaim the spark of excitement you felt when you took those very first steps down your magickal path. The first book of its kind to offer solitary eclectics a solution to the problem of dull or ineffective magick, *The Witch's Bag of Tricks* will help practicing witches renew faith, improve abilities, and cast powerful spells that work. Whether your rituals have become rote or your spells just aren't working, you don't have to settle for magickal mediocrity!

Designed for the experienced eclectic practitioner, this guide offers advanced spellcasting techniques and practical hands-on exercises for personalized magickal development. You'll gain the skills and knowledge you need to custom design your own spells and advance your mystical development. Breathe fresh life into your practice and take your magickal skills further than ever with *The Witch's Bag of Tricks!*

978-0-7387-2633-5, 264 pp., 6 x 9   **$16.95**